A Fly in the Ointment

A farce

Derek Benfield

Samuel French — London
New York - Toronto - Hollywood

© 1996 BY DEREK BENFIELD

CHARACTERS

The Rt Hon Ron Corley MP, Minister for the Environment

Donna, an enthusiastic mistress

Brenda Hackett, a frustrated policewoman

Albert, a devious pizza delivery boy

Louise Corley, a virtuous wife

George Billing, a romantic doctor

It all happens in Donna's bungalow on the Sussex coast of England during a hot summer

ACT I A Friday afternoon
ACT II A few minutes later

Time — the recent past, the present, and (probably) the future!

Other plays by Derek Benfield published by
Samuel French Ltd:

Anyone for Breakfast?
Bedside Manners
Beyond a Joke
A Bird in the Hand
Caught on the Hop
Don't Lose the Place!
Fish Out of Water
Flying Feathers
In for the Kill
Look Who's Talking!
Off the Hook
Panic Stations
Post Horn Gallop
Running Riot
A Toe in the Water
Touch and Go
Up and Running
Wild Goose Chase

ACT I

The living-room of Donna's seaside bungalow in Sussex. It is a hot summer's afternoon

There are three doors in Donna's living-room: one ULC leading to the hall and front door, another to the kitchen DL and the third to the bedroom DR. A large sash window URC looks out on to the street, and there is a large cupboard in the R wall with a small desk below it. Above the kitchen door is a pine shelf-unit with a cupboard beneath it, and a crescent table stands against the wall L of the window. A large comfortable sofa stands RC with a table behind it and an armchair to its L. There is a pleasant, country feel about the bungalow — oak beams, chintzy covers, potted plants and so on

When the Lights come up, the stage is empty. Pleasant sunshine pours in through the window

A door opens, carefully, and a head peers in, its eyes on stalks, looking about. The head belongs to Ron Corley, a slightly balding man in his fifties. Seeing nobody there, Ron comes in, furtively, and starts to search rapidly in various drawers and cupboards, opening and closing them noisily in increasing desperation. The front door slams. Ron freezes in panic, like a startled bird, uncertain what to do. He looks this way and that, a trapped man. He decides to escape through the window and hastens to it. He cannot open it. It is stuck. He pushes at it in alarm

Donna comes in from the hall and with an armful of packages. She is a dark, glamorous, sexy lady in her late thirties

Ron freezes, his face pressed to the window, peering at the glass intently, his back to her

Donna puts down her packages, then turns and sees a man's back facing her from the window. She thinks it is an intruder, and screams

Donna Aaaaah!

Ron turns. Donna recognizes him and smiles, delightedly

Ronnie, my pigeon! You've come back to me! (*She runs to greet him*)

Ron Ah — no.
Donna No?!
Ron No.
Donna (*in disbelief*) *No*?
Ron Not exactly …
Donna But you're *here*.
Ron Yes …
Donna In my bungalow.
Ron Yes …
Donna The bungalow where I live.
Ron Yes …
Donna (*logically*) Then you've come back to me!
Ron No.
Donna You're here, but yet you're *not* here?
Ron I'm here, but I didn't think that *you* were here.
Donna I *live* here.
Ron You go out occasionally.
Donna Yes …
Ron Well, I thought this was one of those occasions.
Donna An occasion when I was out?
Ron Well, you're usually out on a Friday afternoon.
Donna Fancy coming to visit me when I'm out.
Ron I wasn't.
Donna Sorry?
Ron Visiting you.

Donna thinks she knows why he is here, and smiles, happily

Donna Ah! You were bringing me a present and you didn't want me to know! So you chose a day when I wasn't here so you could creep in and leave the present to surprise me. A making-up present! Oh, pigeon, how lovely! (*She looks about*) Now — where is it? Where have you hidden it? (*She races about, looking, then stops and looks at him*) Can't you give me a hint? Am I getting warm?
Ron No — but *I* am …!
Donna Is it a big present or a little present? I can't *see* a big present anywhere … (*Then, suddenly*) It's a motor car! A new BMW! Standing outside! (*She runs to look out of the window, but sees nothing*) No. Nothing out there. Not even a bicycle … Ah! I have it! It's something small! A diamond! A small, delicate, very expensive diamond.
Ron (*horrified*) No! (*He escapes below the sofa*)
Donna *Not* a diamond?
Ron Not anything!

Donna Not *anything?*
Ron No …
Donna Not even flowers? A — a single rose?
Ron No …

Donna's conscience gets the better of her. She covers her face with her hands in shame and runs to him

Donna Oh, pigeon, how could I be so selfish? I don't need a present. You're back, that's all that matters to me! Have you left your bag outside in the hall? I'll help you unpack. (*She tries to lead him away*)
Ron There's nothing to unpack!
Donna Don't be silly, dearest. You took all your clothes with you when you left me. There's nothing of yours still here. Not even a small toothbrush.
Ron I don't need a toothbrush! I'm not staying!

Donna stares at him, frozen for a moment

Donna You said you'd come back to me …
Ron No. That's what *you* said.
Donna You haven't come back to me?
Ron No.
Donna You haven't come back to kiss and make up?
Ron No …

A beat, then she explodes

Donna You *pig*!! (*She attacks him, wildly*)
Ron (*defending himself*) Now, now! Hang on! Hang on! What are you doing?
Donna You broke into my bungalow! I shall summon the Police!
Ron I didn't break in!
Donna This is private property — *my* private property! You have invaded my private property — and that is a crime, even in Sussex. And you know who deals with crime — the Police!

Donna picks up a whistle, pushes open the sash window, leans out, and blows four long blasts. Ron races to her, grabs her hips from behind and tries to pull her back inside. Quite a struggle. Finally he succeeds, like pulling a cork out of a bottle, and they collapse on to the floor, staring at each other, breathlessly

Ron How did you do that?

Donna (*holding it up*) It's a whistle. You blow through it.

Ron The window! You opened the window!

Donna Isn't that what you're meant to do?

Ron *I* couldn't!

Donna What?

Ron I couldn't open the window.

Donna Then how did you break in? (*She gets up, and tidies herself*)

Ron I didn't break in! I came through the front door!

Donna The front door was locked.

Ron I've still got my key. (*He holds up his key*)

Donna snatches the key from him and gives him the whistle

Donna Am I to understand that *that* is the only reason you came here? To return my spare key?

Ron scrambles to his feet, still holding the whistle, grateful for the suggestion

Ron Ah! — Yes! *Yes*! That's it!

Donna So why didn't you post it to me?

Ron (*trying to ingratiate himself*) I — I wanted to be sure you received it, dearest. You know what the post's like in this part of the country. I wanted to deliver it safely.

Donna Then why didn't you simply put it through my letterbox as if you were a postman? There was no necessity to enter my premises and wander about trying to open windows! (*Suspiciously*) Were you ... looking for something?

Ron (*blankly*) What?

Donna You were looking for something!

Ron No! *No*! (*He escapes again*)

She follows

Donna Something of mine that you want? Or something of yours that I've got and you want?

Ron Well, I — I may have left some socks behind. Pale blue, I think ...

Donna If you were looking for what I think you were looking for, you're wasting your time.

Ron Am I?

Donna They're hidden! In a safe place where no casual intruder can find them.

Ron (*innocently*) Wh — what are?

Donna The photographs, pigeon. The photographs.

Ron Wh — what photographs?

Donna The ones I told you about when you left me. The ones of you and me … together.

Ron (*hopefully*) Ah! In the sea in Brighton?

Donna No. In the bed in there! You didn't think I'd leave them lying about, did you? Certain newspapers would pay a lot of money for pictures of the Minister for the Environment in a bedroom with someone who wasn't his wife.

Ron You — you wouldn't do that!

Donna I told you I would.

Ron I didn't believe you.

Donna Oh, yes, you did! That's why you came here today when you thought I was out — to steal those pictures. (*She laughs, enjoying his discomfort*)

Ron You're a blackmailer!

Donna And you're a burglar.

Ron I — I just wanted to avoid any unpleasantness, pigeon …

Donna You should have thought of that before you packed your toothbrush and left me. (*She smiles, sweetly*)

Ron Who the hell took those pictures, anyway?

Donna Oh, I couldn't tell you that! I promised to preserve his anonymity. He's a very keen collector of informal pictures of people in high places.

Ron But how did he take pictures of you and me in your bedroom?!

Donna He's got a very long lens.

Ron has a sudden thought which disturbs him

Ron Wait a minute, though! When those pictures were taken, you … you didn't *know* I was going to leave you.

Donna No. I didn't, did I?

Ron (*deeply hurt*) And you call that romance?

Donna No, pigeon — insurance.

The doorbell rings

Ron Oh, my God! There's someone at the door!

Donna I do have friends.

Ron You'll have to get rid of them!

Donna That wouldn't be very friendly.

Ron (*desperately*) But they mustn't see me! It's Friday afternoon and I'm the Minister for the Environment! Whoever it is — get rid of them!

Ron pushes her out into the hall, abruptly, and closes the door

Donna goes. Whereupon, a small, square, uniformed policewoman in her forties climbs in through the open window. Her name is Brenda Hackett

Ron turns and sees her. He jumps a mile

Aaah!

Brenda I trust I have arrived in time?

Ron What the hell do *you* want?

Brenda I am a policewoman.

Ron I can see that! What are you doing climbing in through other people's windows?

Brenda Responding to an emergency.

Ron What emergency?

Brenda Four blasts of a whistle have been reported by a vigilant neighbour.

Ron Well, there's no emergency here! (*He moves away*)

Brenda (*suspiciously*) Have you been blowing a whistle under false pretences?

Ron I haven't been blowing a whistle at all!

Brenda Then what have you got in your hand?

Ron What? (*He looks to see what he has got in his hand*) Oh — this! It's not mine. (*He puts it down*) *She* gave it to me.

Brenda (*triumphantly*) Ah! A woman! So *she*'s the one who did the blowing?

Ron Mind your own business.

Brenda Did she blow or did she not?

Ron She — she may have blown it once or twice.

Brenda Three or four blasts, I was told.

Ron It was a mistake.

Brenda That's what they all say! In my line of business you get to know where mistakes can lead to. I've known many a man ——

Ron (*quietly*) I'm very surprised to hear it ...!

Brenda — or woman for that matter who ended up in queer street after making a mistake.

Ron Queer street?

Brenda Hot water!

Ron Hot water in queer street?

Brenda If people go around blowing whistles to indicate an emergency when no emergency exists, that's where they end up — without a paddle!

Ron Without a paddle in queer street?

Brenda Up the creek!

Ron That's more like it.

Brenda So where is she?

Ron Who?

Brenda The one who blew the whistle. Hiding somewhere, is she? (*She glances about*)
Ron *I* don't know! It's nothing to do with me.

Brenda suddenly moves in close to him and peers into his face, intently

Brenda Don't I know you?
Ron I hope not.
Brenda I've been trained to remember faces. And I certainly remember this one.
Ron Well, it's never looked at *you* before …
Brenda Do you appear on the small screen? Your face is decidedly familiar.
Ron Not with you it isn't!
Brenda I've seen you reading the news!
Ron No, you haven't.
Brenda I've seen you doing *some*thing.
Ron (*quietly*) I *hope* you haven't …!
Brenda Do you live here?
Ron No.
Brenda Ah! Just visiting!
Ron In a way.
Brenda (*heavily suspicious*) I see …
Ron It's not what you think.
Brenda How do you know what I think?
Ron I can guess …!
Brenda (*grimly*) I'm always running into it …
Ron Running into what?
Brenda Lust! There's lots of it about.
Ron Lots of lust?
Brenda Around every corner.
Ron Well, there's none of it in here!
Brenda You expect me to believe that? I recognize the signs of lust when I see them. And in my line of business you see them all the time. It makes me sick …
Ron Don't you approve of it?
Brenda Of course I approve of it! I just wish it was happening to *me* …!

Donna returns at speed. She stops in surprise, seeing a policewoman, and shoots her hand out, pointing at her

Donna Aah!
Ron It's a policewoman.
Donna And about time, too!

Ron She came in through the window.
Donna (*glaring at Ron*) You've got a nerve! Letting yourself into my property and ordering pizza!

Ron stares at her, blankly, temporarily at a loss

Ron I beg your pardon?
Donna There's a boy at the door delivering pizza.
Ron On a Friday afternoon?
Donna It's a twenty-four hour service.
Ron Well, *I* didn't send for him.

Donna goes to the policewoman

Donna What about you? Did *you* order pizza?
Brenda No. But I am a bit peckish if there's one going.
Donna You took your time getting here! Four blasts! Didn't you realize it was an emergency?
Brenda Ah! So you're the one who did the blowing?
Donna Certainly.
Brenda He had it in his hand when I came in.
Donna What are you talking about?
Brenda The whistle! You blew the whistle and then gave it to him.
Donna Very possibly. Anyway, you're here now, so why don't you arrest somebody?
Brenda (*looking about*) Is there an intruder?
Donna } (*together*) { Yes!
Ron   }   { No!
Brenda There seems to be a difference of opinion.
Donna There is – *some*body ordered pizza! The poor boy was standing out there with a cardboard box steaming in the sunlight.
Brenda The boy?
Donna The box!
Brenda Is he still there?
Donna No. I told him to take the pizza to the people next door.
Brenda Then we must stop him!
Donna Why?
Brenda Because I'm hungry!
Donna You can't eat in the middle of an emergency. You're on duty. You're supposed to be arresting people, not eating pizza.
Brenda But there *is* no emergency.
Donna How do you know?
Brenda (*indicating Ron*) He told me.

Donna He *is* the emergency! He broke into my property.

Brenda (*reluctantly*) Oh, very well. (*She takes out her notebook*) But *I* wouldn't call it an emergency if a man was lusting after *me* …

Donna (*looking about, hopefully*) Where?

Brenda What?

Donna This man — lusting! Where is he?

Brenda (*pointing at Ron*) There!

Donna looks at Ron, doubtfully

Donna This one?

Brenda Yes.

Donna goes to Ron, delightedly

Donna Oh, pigeon — Have you changed your mind and decided to lust instead of loot?

Ron (*glancing nervously at Brenda*) Well — I suppose I could delay my departure for a few minutes …

Donna Oh, good!

Brenda But I was going to arrest you …

Ron Well, you don't have to!

Brenda I want to!

Donna No! I withdraw the charge!

Brenda Then I have no alternative but to leave you alone with this man. The situation here is obviously just as I suspected …

Albert comes in from the hall. He is a bright young man of nineteen, dressed in dark trousers and shoes with a colourfully striped shirt and hat bearing the logo "Pizza Palace". He is carrying a cardboard box, similarly striped, containing a pizza

Albert The people next door say they're not Italians and they can't stand pizza, so this *must* belong to you! (*He sees the policewoman*) Aah! (*He raises his arms in immediate surrender*)

Brenda crosses to him, and peers into his face, suspiciously

Brenda You have assumed the posture of a guilty man. I seem to have arrived in the nick of time.

Albert Am I in danger of arrest?

Brenda That depends on whether you have a satisfactory explanation for your presence here.

Albert I came to deliver pizza.

Brenda How old are you?

Albert May I put my arms down during discussion? I'm not in the habit of holding a pizza above my head.

Brenda Certainly. We don't wish misfortune to befall a perfectly palatable pizza.

Albert lowers his arms, gratefully

Ron (*to Donna*) What's he doing here?

Donna He's delivering pizza.

Ron But nobody ordered pizza!

Albert (*peering closely at Ron*) Do we know each other?

Ron backs away from this unwelcome examination

Ron I hope not. I think I'd have remembered you wearing that hat.

Albert I could have sworn I've seen your face before ... (*He continues peering intently into Ron's face*)

Brenda You haven't answered my question!

Donna (*grumbling*) I wish pizzas and policewomen would disappear. I want to be left alone with my lover ...

Albert Ah! So this is your *lover*? I thought I knew the face! (*He grins, happily, at Ron*)

Ron How do *you* know what her lover looks like?

Albert Well, I've seen you before, haven't I?

Ron Have you?

Albert Oh, yes ...!

Ron (*alarmed*) Where?

Albert Outside here. Getting in and out of cars when I've been cycling past with my evening deliveries. I soon put two and two together. You seem to have become quite a fixture here, haven't you?

Ron No, I haven't! I was just leaving!

Donna But now you're staying.

Ron A–am I?

Donna (*firmly*) Yes, you *are* pigeon!

Albert Now I see you well-lit and in close-up, I definitely know the face. Are you a man in a high position?

Ron I'm above eating pizza, if that's what you mean.

Brenda pulls Albert around to face her, abruptly

Brenda I am in uniform and I expect an answer!

Albert Sorry. I don't recall the question.
Brenda Age!
Albert Oh. Nineteen.
Brenda A modest age. Barely past puberty … (*She sighs*)
Ron (*glaring at Albert*) Even at nineteen he should know better than to deliver pizza to an address where no pizza has been requested.
Brenda What is your misdemeanour?
Albert I haven't got one!
Brenda You raised your hands in surrender at the mere sight of uniform.
Albert It was an instinctive reaction. I have a deep-seated fear of women in authority.
Brenda You must learn to overcome it. Very well. I will ignore it this once. But only — (*she draws in her breath, noisily, through her teeth*) — only in return for pizza.
Albert It'll be cold by now …
Brenda Nevertheless, we cannot let it go to waste. In answering this apparent emergency I have worked up a considerable appetite.
Albert (*nervously*) It may not be to your liking …
Brenda Describe it.
Albert Spinach, tomato, mozzarella cheese.
Brenda Fried egg on top?
Albert Yes.
Brenda Perfect! (*She grabs the box of pizza, starts to go, but hesitates as a thought occurs to her*) Alternatively, you can accompany me to my flat for further questioning.
Ron Your flat?!
Brenda It is but minutes away.
Ron Why not the Police Station?
Brenda I have my own way of handling young boys like this.
Ron I'm sure you have …!
Albert No! Please! Have the pizza!
Brenda (*to the others*) I shall remain within earshot. If a further emergency arises four blasts of the whistle will herald my immediate and speedy return. (*She looks at Albert with a wan smile*) What a pity. You have refused a more stimulating alternative.

Brenda disappears through the window with the box of pizza

Albert watches her go, then turns to the others, forlornly

Albert She never paid me for the pizza …
Ron Think yourself lucky! She would only have paid you in kind.

Donna goes to Albert eager to be rid of him

Donna Well, now you have disposed of your pizza I can see no possible reason for you remaining here. You surely don't intent being privy to me and this gentleman removing our clothes?

Albert (*shocked*) Removing your clothes? It's Friday afternoon! (*He looks at Ron in disapproval*)

Donna Well, *you* were delivering pizzas. I would have thought that gave us carte blanche.

Albert suddenly points at Ron, excitedly

Albert Ah! Got it! You're a politician!

Ron (*alarmed*) What?

Albert I've seen your picture in the papers. My mother always taught me to look at the pictures in the papers. You're the Minister for the Environment!

Ron I have that privilege ...

Albert So *that*'s why you usually arrive here during the hours of darkness? And in a car with tinted windows! The fear of recognition! I've never seen you around here in daylight before. Well, now I know why ...!

Ron Look ... things aren't always what they seem ...

Donna (*quietly*) They soon *will* be! The moment I can get this boy out of here ...

The doorbell rings. They all jump in unison

Ron That can't be anyone we know!

Donna Why not?

Ron Because nobody we know knows we're here.

Albert Oh, my God — it'll be *her*!

Ron Who?

Albert The one in uniform! She'll have returned to pay me for the pizza!

Donna No, no! She would have come in through the window. (*Hastening to the door*) Remain here. I'll make sure that the coast is clear — and then you can get back to Pizza Palace and leave us to get on with more interesting things!

Donna goes, breathless with excitement, closing the door behind her

Ron glowers at Albert, heavy with hatred

Ron You're an observant little bugger, aren't you?

Albert That's hardly fair!

Ron You should have spent more time concentrating on delivering pizza, not car-watching after dark!

Albert My mother always taught me to keep my eyes open.
Ron Pity she didn't follow her own advice and notice your father creeping up on her twenty years ago!

They hear voices in the hall and look at each other in alarm

Ron
Albert } (*together*) Voices!

They race across to listen closely at the hall door. They look at each other again

Ron
Albert } (*together*) Women's voices!

Albert I was right! She *has* come back!
Ron I've a good mind to leave you to her tender mercies.
Albert (*innocently*) Oh, you wouldn't do that, now would you, Mr Minister for the Environment?
Ron You evil little monster!
Albert I'm getting out of here!

Albert hastens to the window. But he cannot open it. It is stuck again. He pushes at it, frantically

I can't open it!
Ron Don't be ridiculous! (*He rushes to assist, but fails also*) How the hell does she do it?

They react to the ladies' voices getting nearer

You'd better hide in here! (*He pulls him across to the bedroom by his ear*)
Albert (*gazing at the door*) Where does it lead to?
Ron What does it matter?
Albert My mother taught me always to ask where I'm going.
Ron It's a bedroom!
Albert (*grinning*) Yes — you would know that, wouldn't you?

Ron hits him across the back of the head, bundles him into the bedroom and comes out again, closing the door. Donna returns, puzzled

Donna It's a lady. For you.
Ron Impossible. Nobody knows I'm here.
Donna Well, she's asking for you.

Ron What does she want?

Donna She said it was a matter of business.

Ron Business? *Here*?

Donna I see you have disposed of the boy.

Ron Oh ... yes. (*His mind elsewhere*)

Donna Then get rid of the new arrival also – and then we can concentrate on more agreeable matters! (*She is near to bursting with anticipation of what is to come as she looks out of the door and calls*) Come along! In here!

Ron Did she give a name?

Donna She said names were of no consequence.

Ron I can't think how anyone knew I was here ...

Donna Well, deal with her speedily! (*She gazes at him in breathless adoration*) Don't be long, pigeon, or I may have to start the preliminaries without you.

Donna darts back into the hall

Ron waits in puzzled anticipation

Louise comes in. She is an attractive, virtuous woman in her forties who at this moment appears to be a little distressed

Ron stares at her, frozen, unable to believe his eyes, a rabbit caught in the headlights

Louise So *this* is where you do it? (*She sniffles into her handkerchief*)

Ron Louise!

Louise (*apparently moved*) Aaaah ... at least you remember my name.

He goes to her, quickly

Ron I — I wasn't expecting you, dearest. (*He looks, anxiously, towards the hall*)

Louise Oh, don't worry. I didn't tell the woman that I was your wife.

Ron Oh, good ...

Louise I thought *you*'d prefer to do that. (*She moves below the sofa*)

Ron This ... er ... this isn't as bad as it looks ...

Louise Oh, I hope not! (*She cries, briefly, then pulls herself together*) The afternoons are a new departure, I presume? I thought you were like a bat and only became active during the hours of darkness.

Ron ignores this barb

Ron H–how did you know where to find me? (*He tries to carry it off*) Ah! Of course! You telephoned my secretary at the House of Commons! She would have explained everything, I'm sure.

Louise Yes. She did. She told me you had gone to have a wisdom tooth removed. I imagine it must have been a very painful extraction if you had to drive to the seaside to recuperate.

Ron She … she's only recently arrived from the typing pool. She tends to make the most elementary mistakes. (*He laughs, nervously*)

Louise No, dearest. It was *you* who did that! I've known for some time that you were up to no good. I'm very susceptible to an aura of guilt. Flowers were arriving for me far too frequently. And then I found these!

Louise produces a pair of brief, frilly knickers from her handbag and plonks them down on the sofa table with a flourish, a hurt and aggrieved woman. Ron stares at them in horror. Quite a pause

Ron (*finally*) W-what *are* they?

Louise Surely you know that? Or don't the ladies of your acquaintance have need of such accoutrements?

Ron They don't belong to me!

Louise I'm very relieved to hear it. It would have surprised me if you had stooped to transvestism.

Ron I don't understand! What have these to do with me?

Louise They were found in the pocket of your Harris tweed jacket when I took it to the cleaners. Imagine my embarrassment! The situation will be the talk of Sketchleys for months to come.

Ron Didn't you tell them they were yours?

Louise They're not.

Ron You could have pretended!

Louise I would have been lying. Anyway, the manageress could tell by my reaction that *I* was not their owner.

Ron Well, I can't think *who* they belong to …

Louise Are there a number of contenders?

Ron I don't know how they got there!

Louise Perhaps someone discarded them in an indiscreet moment and you popped them into your pocket for safe keeping?

Ron You're not suggesting that I —— ?

Louise Yes, that's exactly what I *am* suggesting. And that's why I started to follow you.

Ron Er … f–follow me?

Louise I *am* familiar with the registration number of your car.

Ron (*outraged*) You followed me *here*?!

Louise Yes. On two or three occasions over the past few weeks. You see, I wanted to be sure it was more than just a casual visit before I chose my moment to trap you.

Ron stares at her in horror, unable to believe what he is hearing

Ron *Trap* me? Is that what you're doing?
Louise Certainly! (*With a surprised smile at her own prowess*) And I seem to be doing it rather well ... (*She sits on the sofa, well-pleased*)

A dreadful pause. Then, his mind racing with invention, Ron begins to laugh, nervously, like a machine-gun. A reaction that surprises Louise

Ron Oh, darling! You're so *funny*! Fancy you thinking I was — Oh dear, oh dear, oh dear! (*He laughs and laughs*) Ha! Ha! Ha! Ha!
Louise I'm very hurt that you find it a subject for laughter.
Ron You don't imagine I came here to see Donna?
Louise Who's Donna?
Ron (*pointing, wildly*) Her! The woman out there!
Louise Oh, is that what she's called? We didn't get on to first-name terms standing in the hall.
Ron Fancy you thinking I came to see *Donna*!
Louise An alternative explanation hardly seemed likely.

Ron's confidence is growing as his imagination gets into full swing

Ron Well, well, well! My secret is out ...
Louise It certainly is!
Ron I suppose I'll have to confess ...
Louise (*surprised*) You will?
Ron My secretary was, in fact, not incompetent but well-versed in parliamentary lore.
Louise (*puzzled*) I beg your pardon?

Ron looks about and then bends closer to Louise

Ron Secrecy is essential if a man is to perform his duties satisfactorily.
Louise And I'm sure you did that ...

Ron bears this rebuff with dignity, sits beside her and continues with a casual air

Ron Did you not observe the sea as you drove along?

Louise considers this unexpected change of direction

Louise I had more important things on my mind than maritime life.

Ron presses home his advantage

Ron And during the times you spent observing my car parked outside these premises, you didn't notice the river flowing under the bridge nearby?

Louise Trout were the last thing on my menu ...

Ron Well, there you are, you see! Had you managed to get your mind off wild imaginings and on to realities and observed first the sea and then the river leading *to* the sea, you would have noticed something more disturbing than sexual excess.

Louise Nothing more disturbing springs readily to mind ...

Ron leans forward intently and delivers the coup de grâce

Ron Pollution!

Louise holds his look, at a loss to understand

Louise I beg your pardon?

Ron Pollution ... (*He sighs, sadly*) You talk of trout. Soon there will be none ...

Louise No trout?

Ron And what there are will be floating sadly on the surface. If you had only paused for a moment in your suspicions and looked over the bridge you would have seen that the river is no longer clear and fast-flowing but now resembles a ... a slowly moving ... tide of bubbles ...

An impressive moment. Louise is appalled

Louise And this is due to — to pollution?

Ron nods, sagely

Ron Oh, yes. (*He rises and moves away, well-pleased*)

Louise considers the enormity of the problem for a moment, then has a thought

Louise But this is not an industrial area, dearest. I failed to notice any factories as I drove along.

Ron Because you were under stress! Stress of your own imagining. And, anyway, most of them are ... small ... and hidden away behind the trees.

Louise I think I would have noticed a chimney or two ... What do they manufacture here?

Ron What does it matter?! What*ever* they manufacture there are bound to be by-products. (*Confidentially*) By-products which are being allowed to escape from the factories into the river.

Louise (*astonished*) Really?

Ron Oh, yes. And where does the river flow?

Louise Under the bridge, you said.

Ron (*irritably*) Yes, yes, but after that!

Louise Oh. Er ... (*she thinks*) ... I don't know.

Ron You never were good at geography. (*As to a child*) All rivers flow out to the sea.

Louise smiles, pleased by her scholarship

Louise Oh, yes! I remember *that*!

Ron And what is the result? (*Sadly*) Dear me, what *is* the result ...?

A pause. Ron appears too moved to continue

Louise (*helpfully*) People ... bathing ... in the by-products?

Ron Precisely! Those golden sands that were once a paradise for toddlers will soon be polluted beyond recognition.(*He waits, leaving her time to grasp the enormity of the problem*)

Louise But, Ronnie ... what has that to do with *you*?

Ron tries to control his exasperation

Ron I am the Minister for the Environment! It is my responsibility! (*He returns to his theme*) The guilty parties must be found — and punished — and prevented from further desecration of this once green and pleasant land ... (*He sighs, pleased with his own rhetoric*)

A short pause

Louise But, Ronnie ... what has that to do with you being here in this bungalow with ...? (*She indicates the door to the hall*)

Ron Donna?

Louise Yes.

Ron Ah. (*He smiles, tolerantly, at her slowness of thought*) You little donkey ... (*He kisses her, briefly, on the forehead*) I am using her bungalow ... as an observation post.

Louise considers this for a moment

Louise But what are you observing?
Ron The source of the pollution!
Louise Ah yes. Of course. How stupid I am …

He wanders, warming to his theme

Ron I decided — after thorough investigation of the area — that this was the ideal spot from which to train my binoculars upon the culprits. So I rang this woman's doorbell and put the proposition to her. And I must say, she has been remarkably co-operative.
Louise I'm sure she has …

He ignores this, and continues on his way

Ron I have been preparing a dossier. Names. Places. Photographs of the factories concerned. Times and frequency of by-product emission. (*He sighs*) All this, of course, does take time. Weeks. Months even.
Louise It already has …
Ron (*ignoring this*) And now I have built up an overwhelming case I shall put it into the hands of the Prime Minister. (*He glows with the satisfaction of public spiritedness*)
Louise Put the pollution into the hands of the Prime Minister?
Ron The photographs!
Louise Of course. (*Regretfully*) Oh, dear …
Ron What's the matter?
Louise And all the time I was thinking …
Ron Yes — I know what you were thinking!
Louise My mind sprang so readily to suspicion. (*She hangs her head in shame*)
Ron I know it did, and that was a disappointment to me, donkey.
Louise I should have trusted you.
Ron Of course you should! I am a Member of Parliament and a man of honour.
Louise (*without rancour*) The two things are not necessarily synonymous.
Ron No. No, but in *my* case, dearest, they are.
Louise That's what my heart told me …
Ron Then you must listen to your heart.
Louise And yet my *mind* said …
Ron I know! I know! But you must let your heart rule your mind. It is always the wisest course.
Louise Am I forgiven?

Ron (*generously*) Of course you are, donkey! (*He kisses her, forgivingly, on the forehead*)

Louise But, dearest ... that still doesn't explain how a pair of knickers came to be in the pocket of your tweed jacket ...

Ron looks at her, uncertainly

The bedroom door opens, and Albert looks out. He does not see Louise

Albert Have you got rid of her, then?

Louise looks at him in surprise. And Albert sees her also – and reacts. Louise rises, intrigued

Louise Is this one of your junior ministers?

Ron goes quickly to Albert and strikes him across the back of the head

Ron Go back into the bedroom!
Albert (*indicating Louise*) That isn't the one we were expecting.

Ron hits him again

Louise Were you expecting *another* lady?
Ron No, of course we weren't! (*He hits Albert again*)
Albert He told me to hide in the bedroom.
Louise Did he? Ronnie, it's not like you to go around hiding boys in bedrooms. And dressed in uniform, too! I didn't know you had a secret penchant for the military.
Ron He was hiding from a girlfriend.
Albert She's no girl, and she's no friend of mine!
Louise (*realizing*) Ah! Of course! You're here to keep an eye out for dead fish floating on the river?
Albert (*puzzled*) No, no — I'm from Pizza Palace.
Louise (*her geography reviving*) Isn't that in Florence?
Albert No! It's here! We make pizzas! (*He indicates the logo on his shirt*)
Louise Come nearer. I don't have my glasses on.

Albert exchanges a look with Ron and crosses to Louise. She peers, shortsightedly, at the logo

Oh, I see! So you're in charge of catering?
Albert (*modestly*) Well, I — I deliver the pizzas, yes. On my bike.

Louise Oh, dear. I would have thought that parliamentary catering would have been on a slightly grander scale.

Ron He's nothing to do with me! He's a pizza delivery boy!

Albert Yes. We've got a small business down the road.

Louise I hope *you* haven't been polluting the river?

Albert looks aggrieved

Albert I'd never do a thing like that!

Louise I hope not.

Albert I know it's only a small business, but we do have proper facilities.

Ron strikes him across the back of the head again

Louise Ronnie, do stop hitting the poor boy's head. You'll crack it.

Albert You're not the one who ordered pizza, by any chance?

Louise Sorry?

Albert Spinach, tomato, mozzarella cheese, fried egg on top?

Louise (*appalled at the idea*) No!

Albert Well, you're too late, it's gone, anyhow. (*Moving away, gloomily*) And she never paid me for it …

Louise Who didn't?

Albert The one in uniform.

Louise *Another* one in uniform? Ron, what *has* been going on?

Albert Yes — that's what I'd like to know! (*He picks up the knickers from the table*) Someone seems to have left their knickers on the table.

Louise (*embarrassed*) I'm afraid *I* put them there.

Albert Oh, they're yours, are they? (*He grins*)

Louise No, they are not!

Ron Give them to me! (*He grabs them from Albert and shoves them into his pocket*)

Albert You'd never get into those! They're far too small!

Ron hits him again

Ron Isn't it time you got back to Pizza Palace?

Albert You haven't introduced us yet. (*To Louise*) Are you a friend of his?

Louise (*with a smile*) No. I'm his wife.

Albert is highly amused by this revelation

Albert His *wife*? (*He laughs, noisily*) Did you know that she was —— ?

Ron No, I didn't!

Albert Must have been quite a surprise for you, then.

Ron (*glaring at him*) Yes! (*He controls himself*) Yes — yes, it was … It — it *was*. (*Running to Louise, affectionately*) It was a *lovely* surprise for me, donkey. (*He kisses her, briefly, on the forehead*) Lovely to see you. So … unexpected, and … and lovely. Really *lovely*. Yes …

Louise (*to Albert*) You should have seen his face when I came through that door!

Albert Yes, I'm sorry to have missed that …!

Louise There was a surprise waiting here for *me*, too.

Albert Er … was there?

Louise Oh, yes. You see, I never knew what my husband had been doing here.

Albert Didn't you? *I* did!

Ron Shut up!

Ron tries to hit him again, but Albert is ready for it this time and dodges the blow

The door to the hall opens, and Donna comes in, busily, carrying a thermos flask and a packet of sandwiches. She crosses to Louise, anxious to be rid of her

Donna I've brought you a thermos of soup and a packet of sandwiches for the journey. I'm sure you're eager to be on your way.

Ron Yes, she is!

Louise That's very kind of you, but I think I can stay a little while …

Ron Can you?

Donna That's out of the question! Friday evenings are desperate on the roads leading to and from the coast.

Ron She's right! I think you should go at once!

Albert Yes, I bet you do …!

Donna (*seeing Albert*) I thought you had been disposed of long ago.

Ron Don't worry. I'm going to dispose of him now! (*He glares at Albert*)

Donna (*to Louise*) I'm sure you've had sufficient time to sort out whatever it was you came to discuss, so now you must be on your way!

Ron Yes. The summer evenings in Sussex are surprisingly short. You mustn't run the risk of having to drive home in the gloom.

Louise But I may not be going home ——

Ron ⎫
Donna ⎭ (*together*) What?!

Louise I may decide to stay here ——

Donna Impossible! A certain … (*she quivers gently in anticipation*) … celebration is due to take place here tonight.

Louise A celebration? How lovely! (*Going to Ron*) What is being celebrated?
Ron Don't ask me!
Donna It is a celebration of a ... (*a little embarrassed*) ... of a personal nature. A ... reunion celebration.

Donna smiles at Ron, who is wishing he was at an all-night sitting in the House of Commons

Louise I see ... That *does* sound exciting!
Donna Yes, it is! And an extra female would, I'm sure you appreciate, only prove to be an incumberance.
Louise (*embarrassed*) Oh, I wasn't suggesting that I stayed in your bungalow!
Albert (*quietly, to Ron*) That's all right, then, isn't it, sir?

Ron strikes him

Louise I'm sure they have accommodation in the village.
Ron Not without prior reservation! This is the summer. The place is packed.
Louise In spite of the pollution?
Albert What pollution?
Ron (*grabbing him*) I thought you were going? You should have been back at Pizza Palace long ago! (*He drags him towards the hall door by his ear*)
Donna Perhaps they could go together? (*To Louise*) I'm sure you have no objection to being escorted to your car by a boy in uniform?
Louise It would certainly be unusual ...
Ron He can carry your soup and sandwiches.
Louise Aren't you going to take me out to dinner? I have driven all the way from London.
Ron You don't need dinner! You've got soup and sandwiches!
Donna (*smiling*) It's out of the question, anyway. He's going to be far too busy elsewhere ...!
Albert (*quietly*) He certainly is ...!

Ron pulls him, by the ear, further towards the door

Louise Surely you won't be looking through windows with your binoculars on a Friday evening?
Ron (*nervously*) No — no, of course not!
Donna He'd better not be ....
Albert (*to Ron*) What's she talking about?
Ron Never you mind!
Donna (*to Louise*) So you'll have to continue your business conversation another time.

Albert (*to Ron*) Business conversation? Doesn't she know about your — ?

Ron I thought you were anxious to leave!

Albert Aren't you going to introduce them?

Ron drags Albert by the ear out into the hall and slams the door behind them

Donna hastens to Louise

Donna I apologize if I appear over-anxious for you to go.

Louise That's all right. I quite understand. (*But she sits on the sofa*) What time is he expected to arrive?

Donna Who?

Louise Your ... partner in the ... (*smiling, shyly*) ... celebration.

Donna Arrive? He's already here!

Louise Not the boy in uniform?

Donna No, no, no! A trifle too young for me. Youthful exuberance is rewarding over a short distance, but mature experience is preferable for the marathon.

Louise Oh, dear. If he's already here we mustn't keep him waiting. I'm sure Ron will understand.

Donna I certainly hope so ...! (*She laughs*)

Louise He can always return *tomorrow* with his camera.

Donna (*puzzled*) I beg your pardon?

Louise It is such sad news regarding the river ...

Donna It is?

Louise I'm sure you're very fond of trout?

Donna Well ... lemon sole is my particular favourite.

Louise That, too, will soon be in short supply!

Donna I had no idea ...

Louise But no doubt Ron will be able to reverse the appalling trend once he has got his hands on the photographs.

Donna (*alert, like a bird*) Photographs?

Louise Yes.

Donna (*returning to her*) He *told* you about the photographs?

Louise Oh, yes. He said it was essential for him to get them as soon as possible.

Donna Good heavens! I had no idea they would have such an effect upon the fishing industry ...

Louise As soon as he has the photographs he will show them to the Prime Minister.

Donna is appalled. Even she had not contemplated such a course of action

Donna Is — is that wise?

Louise It is essential. Once the Prime Minister has seen them things will really start to move.

Donna I'm sure they will …!

Louise Heads will roll!

Donna Which ones, I wonder …?

Louise The guilty parties will be exposed. Action will be taken (*Then smiling, optimistically*) And soon trout will once more be swimming serenely in the river …

Donna (*puzzled*) I — I don't think I know what you're ——

Louise Oh, don't worry! I know it's meant to be a secret, and I admire your loyalty, but he has told me all about it.

Donna He *has*?

Louise Oh, yes. And, of course, I've promised not to say a word to anyone.

Donna I'm very glad to hear it …!

Louise After all, it would be disastrous if any of the factory managers found out what was going on before the Prime Minister had been informed.

Donna (*bemused*) Yes, I — I suppose it would …

Louise And I can tell you that I very much appreciate what you've been doing for him these past few weeks.

Donna (*modestly*) It was nothing, really …

Louise I'm sure he was grateful.

Donna Well, he — he has occasionally appeared to be satisfied … (*She smiles, self-consciously*)

Louise I should hope so! He could never have done it without you.

Donna is a little surprised by this

Ron returns, urgently

Donna Ah! You're just in time to see this lady out! (*She pulls Louise to her feet, abruptly*)

Ron Is she going?

Donna (*pointedly*) Of course she is!

Ron Oh, good … .

Donna urges Louise on her way

Donna I'm sure hot soup and sandwiches will sustain you adequately until you reach the environs of civilization.

Louise Thank you. I'm sure they will.

Louise turns to Ron, conspiratorily

As Donna has pressing plans for this evening, I suggest we drive back to London in convoy.

Donna (*laughing*) No, no! *He* can't go!

Louise You surely don't require an audience?

Donna You don't understand ——

Louise He'd only be in the way.

Ron (*nervously*) Perhaps it *would* be better if I went to London ——

Donna (*appalled*) What?!

Ron I can come back first thing in the morning ——

Louise Yes. With his camera and binoculars at the ready!

Donna It will be too late then! I shall have *exploded*!

Ron (*to Donna, desperately*) I can't stay here tonight!

Donna What on earth do you mean? You said that you —— !

Ron propels Louise at high speed towards the bedroom

Ron If you're driving back to London you'll need to powder your nose! (*He opens the door*)

Louise Oh, dear. Is it shining?

Ron Like a beacon!

He pushes her inside

  Louise goes

Ron closes the door, abruptly. Then he grabs Donna and takes her aside a little

  I don't want her to know about *us*!

Donna What does it matter?

Ron She might tell other people! People in Parliament! And that would be the end of my career as an MP. So whatever happens, don't tell her what we've been up to!

Donna But she already knows!

Ron What?!

Donna She even thanked me for what I've been doing for you.

Ron glances, nervously, towards the bedroom

Ron She doesn't *know* what you've been doing for me!

Donna But she said you'd told her all about it.

Ron Ah — yes — well …

Donna You don't have to worry, pigeon. She promised not to say a word to *anyone*, not even the factory managers.

Ron What?

Donna Actually, she didn't seem very concerned. She was far more interested in fish.

Ron I'm not surprised. It's very good for the brain.

Donna Mind you, I *was* surprised that you'd told her about the photographs.

Ron Er ... what photographs?

Donna The ones of you and me! The ones you came here to steal! She said you wanted to show them to the Prime Minister!

Ron What?!

Donna I know I was prepared to give them to the press, but even *I* would think twice about the Prime Minister.

Ron She doesn't know about those photographs!

Donna Yes, she does! She said so.

Ron She was confused.

Donna closes to him, sexily

Donna Anyway, little pigeon, do get her out of the way so we can start taking our clothes off. My engine is beginning to *boil* ....

Whereupon, WPC Brenda Hackett climbs in through the open window, reeling with pleasure

Ron goes to her, urgently

Ron Why are you returning? Nobody summoned you! You were to await four blasts on the whistle before making your reappearance.

Brenda (*breathless*) I *had* to return. I am sated with pizza! (*Relishing the memory*) Spinach, tomato, mozzarella cheese, surmounted by a tender egg. Glorious!

Donna You have no right to climb in through my window twice in one afternoon. Do you have a warrant?

Brenda No. But I am on urgent business. (*She looks about*) Is he still here?

Ron Who?

Brenda The boy! I must find him!

Ron He's gone.

Brenda Just my luck when I've worked up an appetite ...

Ron I thought you were sated with pizza?

Brenda gives him a withering look

Brenda There are other appetites than for food. No, no! I must banish such thoughts from my mind! (*She tries to banish such thoughts from her mind*) But justice must remain impartial. A policewoman must be above accepting

bribes. So I have returned to pay him for his pizza. (*She reacts suddenly, narrows her eyes and peers towards Ron*) How extraordinary ...
Ron What's the matter?
Brenda You seem to have a pair of knickers protruding from your pocket ...

Brenda leans forward, pulls the panties out of his pocket and holds them aloft like a flag. Donna recognizes them

Donna Those belong to *me*!
Ron What?!
Brenda (*heavy with envy*) Just as I thought. Lust around every corner except mine. (*To Ron*) How did they get into your pocket? No! I mustn't ask! I couldn't bear to hear the answer. Sadly, no knickers of *mine* have ever found their way into a gentleman's pocket ... (*She gazes at the knickers, mournfully*)
Ron (*to Donna*) Are you *sure* they belong to you?
Donna Yes, of course! (*Considering deeply*) But I didn't think it was *this* jacket pocket I put them into ...
Ron (*alert like a starling*) What?
Donna I thought it was your Harris tweed.
Ron You — you mean *you* put them there?
Donna Yes, pigeon.
Ron Why?!
Donna (*sulking prettily*) Well, when you said you were going to leave me I was so angry with you! So I put them in your pocket hoping that your wife would find them.
Ron Well, she *did* ...!

The doorbell rings

(*Alarmed*) *More* people arriving?
Donna My bungalow is becoming a thoroughfare! At this rate we'll *never* be able to commence our ... (*she quivers gently*) ... celebration. (*She goes towards the door*)
Ron (*quietly*) Thank God for that ...!

Donna stops, returns to him and grabs his arm

Donna You come with me! (*Laden with desire*) We can start our hors-d'œuvres on the way to the front door ...

Clinging to him like a limpet, Donna takes the distressed Ron out into the hall, closing the door behind them

Brenda suffers, muttering miserably

Brenda Hors-d'œuvres? That presupposes several courses. And *I* have never even reached the roll and butter ...

Louise comes in from the bedroom and is surprised to see a policewoman

Brenda hastily hides the knickers, turning away from Louise

(*To herself*) Good heavens, another woman! The man is obviously insatiable ...

She notices a small china dish on the table. She quickly lifts the lid, drops the knickers into the dish, replaces the lid, and turns to face Louise, clasping her hands behind her back

Louise This place is full of surprises. I go to powder my nose and the bungalow is overrun by police! Are you about to arrest somebody? I had no idea that things had progressed so quickly.

Brenda goes to her, astounded

Brenda You — you *know* the situation here?
Louise Oh, yes. He told me all about it.
Brenda You — you know of the other woman on the premises?
Louise Yes. Apparently she has been most co-operative and is perfectly happy for him to proceed with his operation here. (*She goes to the sofa*)

Brenda is appalled at such condonation

Brenda You mean ... she is aware of *your* presence here today?
Louise Oh, yes. We have discussed the matter fully.
Brenda And you each accept the presence of the other?
Louise Well it is her bungalow. I'm just a visitor. But she has ... (*smiling, confidentially*) ... certain special activities on her mind for tonight – of a more personal nature ——
Brenda Yes! I know!
Louise That's why I'm leaving at any moment. She is anxious to be left alone to start as soon as possible ...
Brenda She has already started!
Louise Oh, I'm sure not ...
Brenda She has already commenced the hors-d'œuvres!
Louise Really? In her present state of anticipation I'm surprised she's

bothering with food. But, tell me, your presence here is surely a little premature? I was under the impression that the Prime Minister had not yet seen the photographs.

WPC Hackett is a stranger to such apparent debauchery

Brenda You — you take … *photographs*?!
Louise Oh, not *me*. I don't know one end of a camera from another. *He* takes the photographs.
Brenda He does?
Louise Oh, yes. Once he has checked the activities with his binoculars.

WPC Hackett is dumbfounded

Brenda I had no idea such things were going on …
Louise Not many people have!
Brenda Sussex is hardly famous for it.
Louise That's why he's been obliged to keep the whole thing secret.
Brenda But — but … *photographs*?
Louise Well, nobody would believe him if he didn't have photographs of what has been going on here.
Brenda And these photographs are going … to the *Prime Minister*?
Louise Oh, yes. Until he has seen the photographs and is fully aware of what is taking place, there can be no further action. That is why I'm rather surprised to see *you* here …

Brenda sinks on to the sofa, appalled

Brenda I have always believed in the integrity of people in high places. It comes as a shock to learn that the Head of State is a party to such goings-on …
Louise (*laughing*) No, no! You misunderstand. The Prime Minister and his cabinet are obliged to give the go-ahead before anything further can happen here.
Brenda The entire cabinet is to see the photographs?
Louise Oh, yes. The government believes in consensus decisions on all matters.
Brenda I don't recall a reference to *this* matter in their election manifesto!
Louise Presumably you are the advance guard? Here to prepare the ground?
Brenda (*blankly*) Sorry?
Louise You are here to plan the offensive? Are you to set up your control centre in this bungalow? I understand it is a convenient location from which to launch your attack when the time comes.

WPC Hackett is totally bewildered

Brenda I am here to pay for my pizza.

Louise stares at her in surprise

Louise Sorry?

Brenda Spinach, tomato, mozzarella cheese, surmounted by a tender egg. Glorious!

Louise Ah! So *you*'re the one who ordered pizza?

Brenda Well, I ——

Louise Is it usual for the constabulary to have food delivered to them in private houses? Surely the local council has sufficient funds to budget for a staff canteen?

Brenda (*a little ashamed*) The pizza was going begging and I was in need of sustenance …

Louise So you're *not* here to —— ?

Brenda No!

Louise Oh, dear. I've been speaking out of turn. What I have told you is highly confidential. Please consider yourself bound by the Official Secrets Act.

Ron staggers in from the hall, breathlessly re-arranging his dishevelled clothing, his hair awry, lipstick on his face

Brenda jumps up. They look at him in surprise. He hesitates, uncertain for a moment of an acceptable explanation. Finally, one occurs to him

Ron The neighbours' dog slipped its leash and has been pursuing me through the shrubbery.

Louise Are you sure your rumpled appearance is not due to some other cause?

Ron I have telephoned the police!

Brenda There was no need. I am already here.

Ron With your mind so firmly set on the pizza delivery boy I doubted your ability to deal satisfactorily with a vicious canine.

Louise Foaming at the mouth?

Ron No. I managed to control myself.

Louise The dog!

Ron I was hardly in a position to notice such details! I was in full flight.

Louise What about Donna?

Brenda (*laughing*) Yes! Was *she* pursuing you also?

Ron This is hardly a matter for levity! If I hadn't been so fleet of foot I could have sustained even greater injury.

Louise Oh, were you bitten, dearest? (*She wipes the lipstick from his face with her handkerchief*)

Ron Yes, I was!

Louise (*sweetly*) By the lady or the dog?

Ron The dog! He nipped me about the ankles as I plunged headfirst into the potting shed and slammed the door.

Brenda But how did you get from the potting shed back to here?

Ron I walked!

Brenda Was the dog not lying in wait for you outside the potting shed?

Ron goes to her, angrily

Ron You're asking a lot of questions!

Brenda It's part of my training.

Ron The dog disappeared! Presumably ... sated by the sight of blood.

Louise Or possibly he found your blood group unacceptable ... ?

Ron gives her a doubtful look

Brenda But what about the person at the front door? Were *they* not involved?

Ron What person at the front door?

Brenda You and the lady of the bungalow went to answer the doorbell. Or had you forgotten?

Ron (*flustered*) Ah — yes. The events which followed quite put it out of my mind ...

Brenda I bet they did ...! What a pity you didn't have your camera at the ready. Your escapade with the dog would have made a diverting addition to your collection.

Ron W–w–what collection?

Brenda The collection of photographs you are going to exhibit before the Prime Minister!

Ron turns to glare at Louise, appalled by her revelation

Ron You've been talking to this policewoman!

Louise I'm afraid I have. But don't worry. I have sworn her to secrecy.

Brenda I had no idea that the south coast of England was a breeding ground for such excesses ...

Ron What are you talking about?

Brenda And neither of them minding about the other! (*She goes to look, briefly, out of the open window, then looks back at Ron*) You don't know, then, who it was who was ringing the doorbell?

Ron Er — no. No. By the time I opened the door and looked out there was nobody there.

Louise Only the dog?

Ron Er — yes.

Brenda (*her hopes rising*) Ah! Then it could have been the pizza boy! I must investigate at once. He may still be close by. (*She climbs out of the window and then looks back at them*) Sex is so unfairly distributed. So much of it in one area and so little in another … (*She disappears down the road*)

Ron (*eager to be rid of her*) You've powdered your nose, then, donkey?

Louise (*moved*) Aah … how nice of you to notice after such a desperate experience in the shrubbery.

Ron Don't let me detain you. I'm sure you're anxious to commence your journey.

Louise So how did they *get* there, then?

Ron (*blankly*) Sorry?

Louise The knickers, dearest. Into the pocket of your jacket at the cleaners. You never told me.

Ron Didn't I? Ah — no — well … er …

Louise You do *remember*?

Ron Of course I remember! (*But he escapes*)

Louise Then tell me.

Ron (*hopefully*) Another time?

Louise *Now*! (*She sits on the sofa, facing him, patiently*)

Ron Now. Right. (*Improvising, slowly*) Well, I … I was in London, you see … walking along Oxford Street. Oh my way to Selfridges, as a matter of fact! I wanted to get ahead with my Christmas shopping.

Louise In August?

Ron Well, you know what I'm like. A hundred and twenty shopping days to Christmas and I start to panic.

Louise Go on.

Ron Well … (*thinking hard*) … as I walked along Oxford Street — on my way to …

Louise Selfridges.

Ron Yes. I suddenly noticed — lying in the middle of the pavement — this … this pair of knickers. Imagine that! Frilly knickers uninhabited in the middle of Oxford Street!

Louise (*horrified*) You didn't pick them up!

Ron Well … yes.

Louise Why? They were nothing to do with you. You should have averted your gaze and walked on like a gentleman.

Ron Ah — yes — well, I would have done. (*A beat*) If it hadn't been for the nuns.

Louise Nuns?

Ron Yes. You know … (*He mimes a nun's wimple*)

Louise How many?

Ron Sorry?

Louise Was it a large group of nuns or just a few?

Ron Oh, just a few. Two, actually. One — (*he mimes*) — rather tall, and the other — (*he mimes*) — rather small. Anyway, they were walking along. Quite quickly, as a matter of fact. Towards me.

Louise Heading for Selfridges?

Ron I didn't ask them where they were going!

Louise So what happened?

Ron Well, I knew as they approached that at any moment they'd be bound to see these ... er ...

Louise Knickers.

Ron Yes. Well, imagine how embarrassed they'd have been! Two nuns coming face-to-face with a pair of frilly panties lying abandoned in the middle of Oxford Street! So I — I swooped down in mid-stride — (*he swoops down to demonstrate*) — picked them up, popped them into the pocket of my Harris tweed jacket — and forgot all about them!

Louise (*smiling with relief*) Aah, so *that*'s how they got there! (*Ashamed*) And there I was thinking that you'd been ... (*She breaks off, gazing at him, fondly*) I'm sorry, dearest. Can you forgive me a second time?

Ron You know, you really must learn to trust me, donkey. (*He kisses her on the forehead*)

Louise Let's throw them away! And I'll never mention them again. (*She reaches into his pocket*)

Ron (*alarmed*) What?

But, of course, they are no longer there

Louise They've gone! Ronnie! What have you done with them?

Ron Ah — well, I ...

Donna strides in from the hall. Her emotional anticipation is now nearing fever pitch. She sees Louise and reacts, impatiently

Donna You're still here! Why are you still here? I gave you soup and sandwiches. You shouldn't still be here!

Louise I was about to leave when Ron came in having been pursued by a dog.

Ron suffers. Donna looks at him with a puzzled smile

Donna A *dog*?

Ron Yes! The one from next door!

Donna I didn't know there *was* a dog next door.

Ron Of course there's a dog next door! Big black dog! Foaming at the mouth!

Louise You said you didn't see if it was foaming at the mouth.

Ron Well, it must have been, mustn't it? Fighting dogs always foam at the mouth. (*To Donna*) It was *here*! Outside the front door!

Donna giggles, and pushes him, playfully

Donna Don't be silly! You didn't go outside the front door …

Ron Yes, I did! And the minute it saw me — it attacked! Anyway, it — it's all over now. I'm still in one piece.

Donna What a relief! Because I'm uncertain how much longer I can contain this overwhelming passion …! (*She sets off towards the bedroom*)

Louise (*quietly, to Ron*) We'd better go …

Ron Ah — yes. Yes — right.

Donna I shall go to bed … to await my lover …

Ron He … he may be a bit delayed.

Donna (*turning*) He'd better *not* be! (*She continues on her way*)

Louise (*quietly, to Ron*) I thought he was already here.

Ron What?

Louise Donna said he was already here. He's probably waiting outside. Unless the dog frightened him off …

Donna (*pointedly*) I hope he's not going to keep me waiting. He wouldn't do that, would he?

Ron No, no, no — I'm sure he wouldn't!

Donna Or change his mind about the … arrangements?

Ron No, of course not! But he — he may have been caught in the traffic! (*He laughs, nervously*) Friday night. From London. You know how it is.

Donna Oh, Ronnie — you've got *such* a sense of humour!

Louise He may not be coming from London.

Donna Oh, yes, he is … . (*She smiles at Ron*)

Ron Well, he … he'll probably have stopped on the way — to buy you some flowers!

Donna hesitates in the bedroom doorway and smiles at Ron, innocently

Donna Well, if he keeps me waiting *too* long — or doesn't appear at all — then I shall simply have to spend my time sorting out those photographs, won't I …?

Donna gives a final, sweet, warning smile and goes into the bedroom, closing the door behind her

Ron is frozen with fear. Louise smiles, warmly

Louise What a sweet kind girl to think of business at a time like this ... I hope you intend to *pay* her for everything she's done for you?

Ron (*grim*) Oh, yes, I'll pay her all right ...! Off you go, then! You can lead the way.

Louise Why? Where are *you* going?

Ron Er ... to — to see if he's waiting outside.

Louise The dog?

Ron The lover! If he's there I'll let him in.

Louise With his flowers?

Ron Yes. So you go out *that* way.

Louise (*surprised*) Through the window?

Ron Well, you don't want to meet him in the hall, do you, donkey? Poor man. He'd be so embarrassed.

Louise All right. I'll wait for you outside.

Ron No, no! You drive on. I'll catch you up in no time. (*He steps quickly out into the hall*) Provided my car doesn't break down ... (*He closes the door behind him*)

Louise looks a little puzzled, but prepared to leave. Then she remembers the sandwiches and thermos flask and returns to pick them up

And at that moment, George Billing looks in through the window, sees her, and climbs in, carrying a bunch of flowers. George is a romantic doctor in his fifties, his eyes a trifle glassy from drink and desire

George Ah! there you are, my partridge!

Louise turns and sees him with some surprise

Louise Dr Billing!
George The very same.
Louise You!
George Yes.
Louise Why are you here? I'm not ill.

George smiles

George I am here for personal not professional purposes.
Louise (*realizing*) Ah! You have brought flowers!
George Forgive my impetuosity. (*He offers the flowers*)
Louise (*with gentle remonstrance*) Dr Billing! You of *all* people!
George Decorum was no match for my desire. (*As she does not take them*) You do not approve of my flowers? Is my selection not to your liking?

Louise Oh, yes! Yes. They're very beautiful ——
George (*smiling, happily*) Your enthusiasm is most gratifying.
Louise Was it you who rang the doorbell?
George I have to confess. Guilty as charged. But my courage failed me and I withdrew with all possible speed.
Louise To the public house, I suspect?
George (*hanging his head*) Alas, yes. They sell courage there by the bottle.
Louise Yes, I thought you'd been drinking a little. I'm surprised at you, Doctor, but I will not detain you from your purpose.
George Sorry?
Louise I am about to leave.
George No! You must remain!
Louise But I have soup and sandwiches for the journey.
George I have other things than sandwiches on my mind.
Louise So I gather! And you mustn't keep the lady waiting! (*She turns away, preparing to go*)

George follows her, anxiously

George My feelings have taken some time to reach the surface. For many moons I have tried to subdue them in the interests of propriety. But passion such as mine cannot be contained indefinitely.
Louise (*turning to him*) Well, the bedroom's through there, so don't let me keep you from your consummation, Dr Billing! (*She starts to go*)

George is a little taken aback by her apparently easy compliance, and he follows her

George Well, I—I was hoping first to enjoy a small aperitif, possibly partake of a delightful meal, a bottle of wine, in a hostelry of your choosing before protesting my passion further.
Louise *My* choosing? What has it to do with me?
George (*smiling, warmly*) Oh, good lady … your modesty is so appealing … What has it to do with you indeed! Did you never suspect?
Louise No, I certainly didn't! You surprise me by your behaviour, Dr Billing. I thought you were a man above reproach.
George Oh, please don't think harshly of me. My intentions are sincere and honourable, but I can no longer hide my deep feelings of love!
Louise Then, as the lady herself is equally anxious, I suggest you waste no more time. I'll take my soup and sandwiches and leave you alone to whatever excesses you have in mind! (*She starts to go again*)
George (*pursuing her*) Alone? Alone? I cannot possibly proceed alone! (*He smiles, saucily*) Shall we commence proceedings by putting these flowers in water before they begin to wilt?

Louise The flowers are no concern of mine!
George No concern of yours? Dear lady, they are from me to you! (*He holds them out again*)
Louise Dr Billing, you are completely out of order. You must give these flowers to the lady you have come to see!

George stares at her, aghast

George But that was my intention! (*He holds out the flowers again*)

With horror, Louise realizes

Louise You — you mean …?
George Precisely!
Louise You have come to see ... *me*?
George Of course! I was convinced that you had already suspected the deep affection in which I hold you.
Louise I — I had no idea! I've only ever seen you in the surgery!
George Where, of course, it was impossible for me to breach our professional relationship.
Louise But … how did you know I was here?
George (*smiling, modestly*) I followed you in my car.
Louise You followed me from London?!
George I fear so. I was hoping that possibly an opportunity would present itself for me to express my feelings in some secluded place away from your husband and the prying eyes of the big city. Imagine my delight when I realized that you had a second home beside the sea!
Louise Oh, my God …! And … and since I arrived here you have been … plucking up your courage?
George (*temporarily annoyed*) And searching high and low for these flowers! Reputable florists are few and far between in this part of the country. (*He hastily resumes his romantic air*) Please accept these blooms from your devoted admirer! (*He goes on to his knees and holds out the bunch of flowers to her*)
Louise Dr Billing, it is out of the question!

The hall door opens

(*Crying out*) Aaah! (*She throws herself upon the sofa, apparently in a sudden faint, and lies there prone*)

Ron comes in

George is still on his knees, facing her with flowers. Ron views the scene, unable to believe his eyes. George remains frozen, looking at Ron in surprise. Ron moves towards them in wonder. Louise stirs, as if recovering consciousness, and looks up at Ron, the brave invalid

Louise Oh, Ronnie — it's you! I — I don't know what came over me. I suddenly felt faint …

Ron accepts this in silence. Then he turns to look, inquiringly, at George, who is still on his knees holding the bunch of flowers

Ron And who are *you*?
George I am a doctor.
Ron Well, you seem to have arrived in the nick of time! (*He turns back to attend to his wife*)

Black-out

CURTAIN

ACT II

The same. A few minutes later

Ron is now sitting beside Louise on the sofa. She is holding a glass of water. George is sitting in an armchair, gazing at his flowers, despondently

After a moment, Ron turns from tending to his wife to look across at George

Ron *You* didn't waste any time, did you?

George Sorry?

Ron Arriving on the scene before the patient even knew she *was* a patient. I had no idea that the National Health Service was so efficient. How did you know that someone was going to be in need of medical attention?

George Ah … Well, as a matter of fact ——

Louise He heard about the dog!

Ron and George are surprised by her vehemence, exchange a look, then both turn back to look at Louise again

George What?

Ron *Dog?*

Louise The one that attacked you! Big black dog. Foaming at the mouth. Probably got rabies! Don't you remember? The doctor heard about it from the neighbours. Didn't you, Doctor?

George D–did I …?

Louise (*to Ron*) So he came at once to give you an injection!

Ron With a bunch of flowers? Where's your little black bag? You can't be much of a doctor turning up without your little black bag.

George It's outside in my car. But I didn't come here for ——

Louise (*hastily*) Then I should go and get it at once, if I were you, Dr Billing!

But George does not take the hint and just looks bemused

Ron Do doctors in Sussex always turn up for house calls with a bunch of flowers for the patient? Must cost a fortune. No wonder there's a shortage of hospital beds.

George (*smiling*) Oh, no! I paid for the flowers out of my own pocket.

Ron So I should think!

George And they're not for a patient. My practice is in London. But, as I'm here, if you like to show me where you were bitten by the dog … (*He gets up in preparation*)

Ron No! No, it … it doesn't matter! It was nothing. He hardly touched me. Who *were* they for, then?

George (*blankly*) Sorry?

Ron The flowers, for God's sake!

George Ah. Yes. Well … (*He lowers his eyes, shyly*)

Louise (*intervening hastily*) Oh, Ronnie! Who do you *think*?

Ron looks at her like a surprised bird

Ron What?

Louise Well … (*She nods towards the bedroom door, knowingly*)

Ron You — you mean … ? (*He nods, similarly*)

Louise Of course!

Ron laughs like a machine gun

Ron Don't be daft! They couldn't be!

Louise Why not?

Ron stops laughing

Ron What?

Louise Well, you did *say* he'd probably have stopped for flowers, didn't you?

Ron Yes, I know I *said* that, but that was because I —— (*He stops just in time*) What?

Louise Well, then … (*She smiles, innocently*)

Ron looks at George, who holds up his flowers with a smile

Ron Ah! So you — you brought flowers for —— ?

Louise Yes! He did!

Ron (*delighted*) Oh, good! (*Quietly*) What a relief …! (*Going to George*) And very nice flowers they are, too. *Very* nice. Well done! (*He shakes the astonished doctor by the hand, vigorously*) Ha, ha, ha! Well, well, well! I'd never have guessed! (*He leans close to George, grinning*) Better be off then and leave you to get on with it, eh? Ha, ha, ha! (*He starts to go at speed*)

George It's quite a relief, I can tell you.

Ron puts on the brakes

Ron What?

George Well … (*he smiles, embarrassed*) … when I first saw *you* … for a
dreadful moment I thought you might be her husband!

Ron Really? Ha, ha! Oh, no! No, no! Far from it! Husband? No! Never! Ha,
ha, ha! (*He starts to go again*)

George So who *are* you?

Ron (*stopping again*) Me?

Louise (*proudly*) He's the Minister for the Environment.

George Then why are you here? Shouldn't you be in your office?

Ron I was just about to go when *you* turned up! (*To Louise*) Right, then! Shall
we — er … ?

Louise Do you think I could have a cup of tea first?

Ron (*impatiently*) What?

Louise I'm still feeling a little faint …

Ron You've got some water!

Louise Yes, but I think sweet tea is what I need.

Ron (*grudgingly*) Oh, very well. The kitchen's through here. But you'll have
to be quick! (*He opens the kitchen door and looks back at George*) I bet
she'll be pleased with your flowers! Ha, ha ha!

Ron goes, laughing, thinking he is off the hook

George gazes at Louise, his eyes limpid with love

George Dear lady, now we are alone …

She goes to him, urgently

Louise Dr Billing, your presence here is intolerable! You must go at once.
If the Medical Council got to hear of your excesses you would run the risk
of incurring the severest penalties.

George But I am a man in love!

*Desperately, George casts himself on to his knees again and thrusts out the
flowers once more*

Louise Ssh! I will endeavour to keep the Minister for the Environment in the
kitchen for a few minutes. A cup of tea and a digestive biscuit should do
the trick. In the meantime, you must retreat through that window and return
speedily to the anonymity of your surgery.

George But my flowers … ?

Louise Take them with you!

Louise disappears, quickly, into the kitchen and slams the door behind her

George remains on his knees, a picture of thwarted passion

> *The bedroom door opens and Donna comes out, impatiently. She is now wearing a delightful négligé*

Donna If you don't join me soon I shall start on my own!

Donna stops, seeing a small stranger kneeling down with a bunch of flowers. George sees her also. They remain motionless for a moment, staring at each other

Donna Are you in prayer?
George I wasn't. But it may come to that.
Donna Then why are you on your knees?
George I — I was hoping to see someone.
Donna They would be surprised to find you in that position. Are you searching for something?
George Waiting.
Donna Waiting?
George Alas, in vain.
Donna Then we have something in common.
George You were waiting also?
Donna Yes. And also, it seems, in vain. Do you intend remaining on your knees indefinitely?
George No, no! I do apologize! (*He scrambles to his feet*) I don't usually kneel in the presence of ladies. Unless I intend proposing marriage, of course.
Donna I presume that is not what you had in mind as we have only just met? I've never even seen you before.
George I am a stranger.

Donna is enchanted

Donna A stranger with flowers! At least you have *something* in your favour.
George I came from London.
Donna Another person from London? Good heavens! The city must be deserted. I'm surprised your flowers haven't wilted after such a desperate drive.
George Oh, no! I purchased the flowers locally.
Donna How very sensible.
George (*his annoyance returning briefly*) And I had to search high and low! Reputable florists are few and far between in this part of the country …
Donna And how did you get in here?

George Through the open window. I am a doctor.

Donna Is someone here in need of treatment?

George Apparently not.

Donna Then you have had a wasted journey.

George It *is* beginning to look that way …

Donna Tell me … isn't it a little unusual for a doctor based in London to have patients as far afield as the Sussex coast? That seems to be spreading the resources of the National Health Service rather thinly.

George Oh, I have no patients here.

Donna Then what is the purpose of your visit?

George lowers his head, modestly

George I am here … for pleasure.

Donna So am I. And it seems as if we are both destined for disappointment.

George (*unhappily*) There are more people here than I anticipated …

Donna And you are adding to the numbers! Why are you searching for pleasure in the sitting-room of my bungalow?

George looks astonished

George *Your* bungalow?

Donna Yes.

George Are you quite sure?

Donna I hope you don't expect me to produce documentation at such short notice?

George I … I thought the other lady was ——

Donna (*rather put out*) You mean she's still here?

George Oh, yes. In the kitchen having a pot of tea.

Donna I've already provided her with soup and sandwiches! Some people are never satisfied.

George The Minister for the Environment is officiating with the tea-bags.

Donna (*cheering up*) Ah! He's still here, then? That's something. (*A sudden thought*) Is your search for pleasure directed against anyone in particular?

George Certainly! I'm not indiscriminate with my passion.

Donna (*suspiciously*) Your flowers have a certain … flamboyance. I hope the object of your affection is not someone in high office?

George What are you suggesting?

Donna Well, apart from yourself, there are only three people here at present. I eliminate myself as an object of your desire on the grounds that we have only just met. I simply wish to establish for which of the other two you have brought flowers.

George (*appalled*) For the lady, of course!

Donna What a relief! The thought of fighting with a London doctor over the same man is more than I could bear. (*She moves away from him*)

George Am I to take it that you are married to the Minister for the Environment?

Donna No! Certainly not! Not married …

George (*smiling*) Ah! I see …

Donna Precisely! (*She giggles*)

WPC Hackett climbs, urgently, in through the open window

Brenda I understand there is a criminal at large.

Donna My window is fast becoming a right of way …

Brenda An alert neighbour spotted a man entering your bungalow through the open window carrying a bunch of flowers. (*She looks about and sees George holding a bunch of flowers*) Ah! That would be you? (*She joins him*)

George I have a bunch of flowers, certainly …

Brenda And you entered via the open window?

George I rang the doorbell, but nobody answered.

Brenda So you took advantage of an open window?

George I was anxious not to waste any time.

Brenda (*suspiciously*) So speed was of the essence?

George Certainly.

Brenda looks back at Donna

Brenda I'm surprised to find *you* in a vertical position! I assumed that by now you would have finished the hors-d'œuvres and the fish and be well into the main course!

Donna So did I …!

Brenda turns to George again

Brenda Give those to me. (*She grabs the bunch of flowers and begins to examine them, peering closely amongst the stems*)

George What are you looking for?

Brenda Hidden arms. There may be a gun in here. (*She finds nothing*) No … So what is the mystery of these flowers? (*She thinks, deeply*)

George There is no mystery!

Brenda If not to hide a gun then what? (*A sudden thought*) Ah! Drugs! Opium! And yet these blooms do not resemble poppies … I have it! To lull the local constabulary into a false sense of security! Who would think a man had criminal intentions if he is seen carrying a bunch of flowers?

George I bought them locally.

Brenda You expect me to believe that?

Donna He would hardly carry flowers all the way from London.

Brenda Is that where he came from?

Donna Apparently.

Brenda No country amateur, then! A polished city professional. Have you searched the premises? Is anything missing? Has he a van parked outside awaiting the antique furniture? (*She goes to look out of the window*)

George (*following her*) I'm not a criminal. I'm a doctor.

Brenda So was Crippen, but that did not deter his evil intent.

Donna hastens to her

Donna Officer, you misunderstand. The doctor is not here to steal. He is here in the cause of love.

WPC Hackett bridles like a frightened horse

Brenda Love?! (*She looks at George, accusingly*) Love?

George (*romantically*) Love …

Brenda A doctor in love?

Donna That's why he was carrying flowers.

Brenda I might have guessed! Lust around every corner. (*To Donna*) So now you have two lovers? What an unfair distribution of the available resources. Now I know why you were in such a hurry to commence your activities with the other one — you had a *queue* of men waiting in the sitting-room!

Donna No, no, no! The doctor isn't here to see *me*!

Brenda Really?

Donna Of course not.

Brenda (*to George*) Is this true?

George Certainly. I had no idea this lady was in the bungalow.

WPC Hackett considers this, and becomes hopeful

Brenda Have you already selected the lucky recipient of these flowers or are you open to suggestion?

George Oh, yes! I have chosen the lady.

Brenda What a pity …

George I have admired her for some time. And today finally plucked up courage to follow her from London and express my feelings for her here in this bungalow.

Brenda looks at Donna, suspiciously

Brenda I hope you're not renting out your property for shady purposes. If so, I shall be obliged to arrest several people.

Donna I had no idea the doctor intended to declare himself in my sitting-room!

Brenda (*to George*) And has this declaration to the lady already taken place?

George Oh, yes …

Brenda Well, you appear to have frightened her off.

George She's in the kitchen.

Brenda reacts to this as if it was a deep revelation of decadence

Brenda *Hiding* in the kitchen? And I suppose you are to go and find her? You are to search for her … slowly and silently … in every corner … and in every cupboard … until she finally surrenders. (*She shudders at the thought*) So *this* is what is meant by foreplay …

George She felt in need of tea.

Brenda I'm not surprised! The sudden appearance through an open window of a London doctor bearing flowers and exuding passion would be enough to startle the most balanced of women! Hot sweet tea would be an absolute necessity.

Ron walks in from the kitchen

Donna comes down, giving him a hard look

Donna About time, too! I was about to start sorting the photographs …

Ron (*triumphantly*) Well, you don't need to do that now, do you?

Donna Sorry?

Ron (*seeing Brenda*) Why have you returned?

Brenda I was told there was an emergency, but on arrival I find it is yet another case of lust!

Ron So I gather! (*He crosses to Donna with a big smile*)

Donna What …?

Brenda And you don't object?

Ron Certainly not! I'm delighted!

Brenda Decadence seems to know no bounds in this part of the country.

Ron (*to Donna*) We're going to leave you two together! Ha! Ha! Ha!

Donna (*puzzled*) Sorry?

Brenda moves down to Ron

Brenda Has the sweet tea assisted her in getting over the shock of seeing this London doctor appear through the open window like Peter Pan?

Ron London doctor? You mean he isn't a local locum?

Brenda No. He's driven here specially.

Donna (*suddenly activated*) There are far too many people in this bungalow! I was hoping it would just be two consenting adults in private …

WPC Hackett glares at Ron

Brenda I presume you have your camera at the ready? This doctor is another likely subject for your licentious lens!

George I don't think I want my picture taken …

Ron Haven't you given her your flowers yet? If you go on clutching them like that they'll start to wilt. (*He grabs the flowers from George and thrusts them, delightedly, at Donna*) There you are!

Donna Don't thrust other people's flowers at *me*!

Ron How can you be so ungracious? The poor man had to search high and low! Reputable florists are few and far between in this part of the country …

Donna He didn't bring them for me!

Ron Oh, you don't have to pretend! I know all about it. I might have guessed you'd have another one on standby! (*Slightly aggrieved*) And I'd only been gone a week …

Donna What are you talking about?

George Can I have my flowers back?

Ron Oh, all right. (*He takes the flowers back to George*) Trying to keep your passion a secret, are you?

Brenda (*to George*) It won't be a secret for long if he shows pictures of you to the Prime Minister!

George (*wide-eyed*) Is that his intention?

Brenda Oh yes! Apparently they're going to pass them around during Cabinet meetings.

George Oh, Well, that's very flattering, of course. But I doubt if the PM would be interested. I am, after all, only a humble GP and not, I fear, as photogenic as I might be.

Brenda Don't worry. They won't be looking at your face!

Donna (*keen to be rid of him*) Doctor, why don't you take your flowers out into the *kitchen*? (*She smiles, encouragingly*)

The doctor cheers up at once and takes the flowers

George Well, if you're quite sure you have no objection to my declaring my passion under your roof! (*He goes out into the kitchen, smiling optimistically*)

Brenda I can only assume that he's in private practice. Such desire would never be found lurking beneath the surface of the NHS.

Ron Isn't it time you returned to duty? The crime rate in Sussex must be rising by leaps and bounds in your absence.

Brenda looks at him, stonily

Brenda I see you're anxious to be left to continue your search for pleasure. I am appalled to know that the Prime Minister has given his blessing to such excesses. I may have to reconsider my political allegiance.

Ron What are you talking about?

Brenda No, no! I can bear the language of lust no longer. I shall return to the station house and immerse myself in the pursuit of crime.

Brenda climbs out of the window and disappears down the road

Donna goes, quickly, to close the window, relieved to be rid of her, and returns to Ron with a big, sexy smile

Donna Now …!

Ron No!

Donna We're alone …

Ron We're *not*!

Donna Just the two of us. Isn't that a wonderful arrangement? You be the man and I'll be the woman.

Ron No, no!

Donna All right, we'll try it the other way for once. (*She tries to pull him towards the bedroom*)

Ron I'm not going in there with you!

Donna You never used to object.

Ron Donna — that's all over now!

Donna Oh, pigeon, my engine's beginning to overheat … Come on! What's one more drop in the ocean? (*She starts to pull his shirt out of his trousers*)

Ron (*resisting, valiantly*) Surely you can wait until the doctor comes back?

Donna The doctor didn't drive all the way from London just to watch you taking your clothes off.

Ron I'm not taking my clothes off!

Donna Oh, yes, you are!

Ron No!!

Ron escapes around the sofa, trying to adjust his clothing. Donna follows him, smiling in breathless anticipation

Donna And as you've kept me waiting so long I'm going to skip the hors-d'œuvres and the fish and go straight on to the main course! (*She lunges at him, hungrily*)

Ron How can you carry on like this when your new lover's waiting out there in the kitchen?!

Donna I haven't *got* a new lover!

Ron The doctor! The doctor!

Donna The doctor's nothing to do with *me*!

Ron He brought you flowers!

Donna They weren't for me — they're for *her*!

Ron (*frozen*) What?

Donna The one who came to see you on business! The doctor's in love with her!

Ron What! (*He backs towards the kitchen*)

Donna (*closing to him again*) So why don't we forget all about it being over between us …? (*She puts her arms around him and clings on like a limpet*)

Ron resists. But it is not easy

Ron No, Donna — no! I — I left you last week … Are you *sure* about the doctor? (*He glares at the kitchen door*)

Donna (*kissing his face*) The newspapers would have a field day with those photographs … I can see the headlines now — "Environment Minister in seaside sex scandal!"

Ron You — you wouldn't do that!

Donna Not if you stop all this talk about leaving me, pigeon … (*She starts to unbutton his shirt*)

Ron Oh, my God …!

They struggle

> *Albert looks in through the window and sees them. He grins and knocks on the glass, rat-a-tat*

Ron and Donna turn and see a grinning face at the window

Donna These constant interruptions are doing dreadful things to my libido. Who is it?

Ron It's that bloody pizza delivery boy!

Donna pushes him away, angrily

Donna How can you think of food at a time like this?

Ron I didn't send for him! (*Quietly*) But I'm jolly glad to see him …

Donna Well, get rid of him! (*Then she smiles, sexily*) I'll keep my passion simmering on the back burner …

She slides out into the bedroom

Ron goes to the window. He cannot open it. It is stuck again. He pushes at it

Albert joins in from outside

Both jump up and down in unison with their efforts. But they cannot move it

Ron sighs and goes into the bedroom. From within we hear the delighted sound of Donna's welcome

Donna (*off*) Aaaah, pigeon .... (*A pause, then abruptly*) *What*?!

Donna walks out of the bedroom, furiously, an ashamed Ron in her wake. She has no difficulty in opening the window immediately. She marches back into the bedroom, glaring at Ron as she passes him, and slams the door behind her

Albert climbs in through the open window. Ron goes to him, trying to fasten the buttons of his shirt as he does so

Ron We didn't order pizza!
Albert I presume your wife is no longer in the vicinity?
Ron What gave you that idea?
Albert Well ... you seem to be on the verge of abandoning your clothes ... you wouldn't be doing that if your spouse was anywhere in the Sussex area, now would you?
Ron Well, she *is*, as a matter of fact! (*He paces away, desperately, below the sofa*)

Albert follows him in disbelief

Albert Still in the town?
Ron Still in the kitchen!
Albert *What*?!
Ron Ssh!

Albert whistles a note of deep admiration

Albert You don't half live dangerously. I suppose that's all part of your parliamentary training? My mother was right, then.
Ron What the hell's it got to do with your mother?
Albert She always told me that if ever I occupied high office in Government, I'd have to learn to be quick on my feet. (*He executes a neat step*)

Ron Your mother's a mine of useless information.

Albert You never know. It might come in handy one day … Is that why you were struggling a bit, then? I thought you didn't have your mind one hundred per cent on the job. That would be on account of the marauding marriage partner, eh? (*He chuckles*)

Ron Yes! Of course!

Albert (*indicating the bedroom*) So *this* one still doesn't know that (*indicating the kitchen*) *that* one is your wife?

Ron Of course she doesn't!

Albert And … (*indicating the kitchen*) *that* one doesn't know that (*including the bedroom*) *this* one is your —— ?

Ron I *hope* she doesn't …!

Albert (*thoughtfully*) It's a funny thing, but you don't strike me forcibly as the gigolo type somehow. But then I suppose they do come in all shapes and sizes …

Ron Is that something *else* your mother told you?

Albert's devious mind is now working overtime

Albert Of course … you being the Minister for the Environment and all that … with responsibility in high places … I don't suppose you'd want — (*indicating as before*) — *that* one or *this* one … to find out about *this* one or *that* one …?

Ron glares at him, suspiciously

Ron What are you suggesting?

Albert Well … I mean … (*He shrugs*)

Ron grabs him by the lapels and pulls him close to his chest, abruptly

Ron Is that what you came here for? Is that what's been going through your devious little mind?

Albert My mother said …

Ron Never mind what your mother said!

Albert sighs, regretfully

Albert Well, be fair, sir … there *is* a bit of a recession in the pizza delivery business at the moment. Not a lot of money about. (*He shrugs, helplessly*)

Ron glares at him for a second

Ron You're an avaricious little bugger, aren't you? (*He pushes him on to the sofa abruptly and goes towards the bedroom, his mind racing*) You'd have to do more than just keep quiet.

Albert is puzzled, not knowing what Ron is getting at

Albert Sorry? I … I don't quite …?
Ron (*returning to him, ominously*) If I give you money, you horrible little toad, you'll have to *earn* it!
Albert And what will I have to do to earn it?
Ron You'll have to go in *there*, won't you?
Albert (*leaping up in alarm*) Into her bedroom?!
Ron (*stopping his mouth*) Ssh! Why not?
Albert No fear!

Albert tries to escape, but Ron grabs him and pulls him back, abruptly

Ron I thought you were worried about the recession? You'd have to deliver a hell of a lot of pizzas to improve *your* balance of payments! (*He produces a ten-pound note and holds it out to Albert*)

Albert Only ten quid to go into her bedroom? You must be joking!

Ron hastily produces another ten-pound note. Albert takes the money, better pleased, stuffs it into his pocket and starts to go towards the bedroom. Then he stops and looks back at Ron, uncertainly

But what am I supposed to do when I *get* in there?
Ron What abysmal poverty of mind … Act as a decoy, of course!
Albert A what?
Ron A distraction! Take her attention away from me! (*He sighs, impressed by his own fatal attraction*) I keep telling her that it's all over between us, but she refuses to take no for an answer.
Albert Oh, I *see*! And you think she might prefer a younger man?
Ron Well, I wouldn't put it quite like that … .
Albert And if *that* one (*indicating the kitchen*) thought that *this* one (*indicating the bedroom*) was interested in *this* one (*indicating himself*) then you'd be in the clear with *that* one (*indicating the kitchen*)?

Ron shrugs, innocently

Ron Well, what's wrong with that?

Albert draws in his breach, doubtfully

Albert Ooh … I'll have to think this over …
Ron Well, don't take too long about it or she's liable to explode!
Albert I wonder what my mother would have said …
Ron I'm not asking your mother to do it!
Albert I think she'd have said that it was worth more than a couple of tenners!

Ron glares at him, but realizes that he has no option. He digs out another note and hands it over, grudgingly. Albert puts the money into his shirt pocket and sets off, apprehensively, towards the bedroom. Then he stops and looks back at Ron

Do you think I should keep my uniform on?
Ron Of course you should! You can't enter a lady's boudoir stark naked. Do have some finesse. (*He thinks of something*) Here — wait a minute!

Ron takes some flowers out of a vase, wraps them in a piece of newspaper, and hands the bouquet to Albert

How about that?

Albert takes the flowers, deeply impressed

Albert Oh, yes …! A nice touch, sir. That should do the trick. I can tell you went to a good school.

Albert plucks up courage and goes into the bedroom, closing the door behind him

A pause. Ron waits, hopefully. Then, assuming all is going well, he grins in happy relief and is about to set off towards the kitchen when the bedroom door opens, abruptly

Albert is ejected at high speed like a rocket, still clutching the flowers. He trips and falls to his knees in front of Ron

Ron (*gazing down at him, appalled*) Well?

Albert stares up at him, disconsolately

Albert She says she wants the organ-grinder not his monkey.

Ron (*fed up*) You hopeless fool …! Right! (*He holds out his hand*) Give it back to me.

Albert holds out the flowers

Not the flowers, you idiot! The money!

Albert Why should I give you the money?

Ron Because you failed! I didn't give you the money to fail!

Albert My mother would say that the money was a non-returnable advance that didn't depend upon success or failure …

Ron Give it to me!

Ron tries to get the money out of Albert's pocket, and they are struggling, Albert still on his knees holding the bunch of flowers, Ron with his shirt still hanging out

Louise walks in from the kitchen and sees them

Louise Ronnie!

Ron and Albert freeze

What on earth are you doing?

Ron cannot think what he was doing. Albert tells the truth, as his mother would have wished

Albert He was trying to get his money back.

Louise I can't think why he gave you money in the first place. You didn't order pizza, did you, darling?

Ron Of course I didn't!

Albert He asked me to do something for him.

Ron (*glaring at him*) Shut up! Shut up!

Louise So why does he want his money back?

Albert Because I didn't do what he wanted me to do.

Louise Oh, what a pity …

Albert I'm not very good at that sort of thing. I haven't had a lot of practice.

Louise Ronnie dear, your growing obsession with boys in uniform is becoming increasingly disturbing.

Ron He's nothing to do with me!

Louise Then why is he on his knees offering you flowers?

Ron (*glaring at Albert again*) Get up! Get up!

Albert scrambles to his feet, still clutching the flowers. He holds them out to Ron

Albert You going to take these or not?
Louise Oh, go on, dearest, take them if it'll make him happy.

Ron grabs the flowers, roughly

Ron He wasn't giving the flowers to me!
Albert No. *He* gave them to *me* ...

Ron hits him on the head with the flowers, then casts them on to the sofa

Louise So that's what has been going on in here ...
Ron (*hastily counter-attacking*) Never mind what's been going on in here! What's been going on out *there*? (*Indicating the kitchen*)
Louise Sorry?
Ron You and your doctor!
Albert (*surprised*) Doctor?
Louise We've been putting his flowers in water.
Ron *His* flowers? *Your* flowers!
Louise They're not my flowers!
Ron He brought them for you! And he had to search high and low! Reputable florists are few and far between in this part of the country ...
Louise W–why should he bring me flowers?
Ron Because he's in love with you!
Louise Don't be silly, dearest ...
Albert *I* didn't even know there was a doctor present ...
Ron Will you keep out of this? (*Turning to Louise again*) He said he was going to declare his passion in the kitchen! And that's where *you* were!
Albert Oh, that's all right, then, isn't it? She's got one of her own ...
Ron Shut up!
Louise He was only having a cup of tea.
Ron I've only your word for that!
Louise And now he's going back to London.
Albert Bit of a wasted journey for him, then.
Ron Will you be quiet?!
Louise Ronnie — your clothes seem to be in total disarray ...

Ron is caught on the wrong foot

Ron What?

Louise Look at your shirt! Don't tell me that dog's been chasing you again?

Ron hastily starts to tuck his shirt in again

Donna comes out of the bedroom and sees Albert

Donna Ah! He's still here! I assumed you'd have gone by now! (*Advancing on him*) How dare you enter my bedroom uninvited?

Albert takes cover behind Ron

Ron He thought you'd be pleased.
Donna Well, I'm not! (*She sees Louise*) Why aren't you in the kitchen? Don't tell me you've spurned the doctor's advances and nipped his passion in the bud?
Louise I certainly have! He is already preparing to leave for London.
Donna Then you must follow him immediately! (*Quietly to herself*) These constant interruptions are playing havoc with my sex life … (*Turning to Ron*) Get that boy out of the way and back to his pizzas!
Ron But he loves you!
Albert No, I don't!
Ron Yes, you do! (*He thrusts another note into his hand*)
Albert Yes, I do!
Ron Well, tell her, then! (*He pushes Albert towards Donna*)

Donna reacts with distaste at his sudden proximity and pushes him aside on to the sofa

Donna Out of my way!! (*She grabs Ron and embraces him, recklessly*) Pigeon, I can wait no longer! I am about to *explode*!
Ron Then take him! Take the pizza boy!

Albert cowers on the sofa

Donna Pizza boys are of no avail to a woman on the brink of passion! You must keep me waiting no longer! (*She embraces him, wildly*)
Ron (*to Louise; struggling*) She is ill! She hallucinates!
Donna Follow me to the bedroom this minute or I may reach the summit alone!
Ron No! No!
Donna Then I shall throw myself to my death from the window!
Ron You can't. It's a bungalow. (*To Louise*) Fetch the doctor! She is in urgent need of sedation!

Louise But the doctor's gone!

Albert I think *I*'ll go, too … (*He starts to go*)

Ron You stay where you are! You may yet be playing a major role in the proceedings.

Ron escapes from Donna's clutches, and goes to Louise, urgently. Donna casts herself, moaning, on to the sofa

He can't have gone far! Bring him back! Tell him he's needed urgently to calm a woman on the brink of hysteria!

He pushes Louise out into the hall

Louise goes

Ron closes the door

Donna Oh, why didn't I buy a house instead of a bungalow … .

Ron What?

Donna Then I could have thrown myself from a higher window!

Ron You don't have to go as far as that!

Donna Good! Then let's go as far as the bedroom! (*She starts to go, dragging him with her*)

Ron I can't! I mustn't!

Donna Then I shall cast myself into the river! (*She heads for the window*)

Ron I wouldn't do that. It's polluted.

Ron hastens after her. He grabs her from behind as she tries to get out of the window. Donna struggles to free herself from his clutches

Donna Leave go! I wish to die!

Ron (*to Albert*) Don't just stand there! Give me a hand!

Donna's face turns, quickly, to look back into the room

Donna He'd better not bring his hand anywhere near me! (*She continues to struggle*)

Ron But he loves you! He said so! (*To Albert*) Come on!

Albert I don't have to touch her, do I?

Ron Of course you have to touch her!

Donna He'd better not!

Ron She's going to jump into the river!

Albert I don't think I want to touch her.

Ron Then add your weight to mine! I can't manage alone!
Albert Oh, all right …

Albert puts his arms around Ron's waist and assists him in trying to pull the struggling Donna back inside. A noisy contest, Ron shouting encouragement to Albert, Donna moaning

Ron Heave! Heave! Heave!

Finally, Donna releases her hold on the window and they all fall back on to the floor. They sort themselves out

   Donna runs out into the bedroom, moaning

Donna (*as she goes*) Aaaaaaah …!

Ron and Albert gather their breath

Ron You see the effect I have on women?
Albert (*wide-eyed*) Has she gone mad?
Ron That's passion, boy. Passion. Don't the girls in Pizza Palace behave like that when you say no to them?
Albert I never say no to them.
Ron Oh, you have *had* experience of girls, then?
Albert Yes, but this one's a bit out of my class. I'll need danger money if I have to face up to her again …
Ron You've already had forty pounds!
Albert My mother would say that …

Ron quickly shoves another note into his pocket. Albert smiles, delightedly

   I think passion's going to be more profitable than pizza …

Donna returns with a length of rope, and heads towards the hall

Ron Where are you going?
Donna To hang myself from the banisters!
Ron You haven't *got* any banisters.
Donna (*stopping*) Oh, damn! (*She sinks into the armchair, despondently*) A bungalow is no place for a woman contemplating suicide. (*She casts the rope aside and considers her next move, gazing into space*)
Ron (*hissing at Albert*) Go on, then! Now's your chance!

Ron pushes Albert towards Donna, who is unaware of his approach. Albert looks back at Ron, short on courage. Ron gestures, encouragingly. Albert drops, suddenly, on to one knee beside Donna

Albert *Darling!*
Donna (*jumping a mile*) Aaaaah!

Albert lunges at her, desperately. She leaps up out of his clutches and rushes to the window

(*Calling*) Rape! Rape! Rape! (*She picks up the whistle, leans out of the window and blows four sharp blasts*)

Ron and Albert race across to her. Ron grabs her from behind, with Albert's arms around his waist, assisting as before. They try to pull her back inside

Ron Heave! Heave! Heave!

The hall door opens. Louise and George come in, urgently. She is carrying his black bag, and he is holding a syringe at the ready. They stop and view the scene in surprise

Louise Ronnie!

The three figures at the window turn and see the newcomers. Donna releases her hold on the window and they all collapse on to the floor like a pack of cards. Ron scrambles to his feet and goes to George

Ron Ah! Doctor! Once again you appear in the nick of time. (*Indicating the syringe*) Is that thing loaded?
George Yes, but I have no authority to administer sedatives in Sussex.
Ron This is no time for niceties! It's an emergency! (*He urges the doctor towards Donna*)

Donna is getting to her feet and sees George approaching. She looks surprised

Donna Doctor! I see you have returned to declare your passion a second time. Well, please do it in the kitchen. It's far too crowded in here.
George (*to Ron, uncertainly*) Is this the patient?
Ron Yes! Get on with it!
George She doesn't appear to be in need of sedation ...

Donna Forgive me if I don't engage you in further conversation but I am in the middle of escaping from rape and attempting suicide. Aaaaah! (*She races back to the window*)

Ron and Albert hasten to retrieve her before she can climb out of the window

Ron Doctor, don't stand there dithering!
Donna Let me go! Let me go! I will not be manhandled!
Albert (*to Ron*) I thought that was what she wanted.
Ron Come on, Doctor! Speed is of the essence! This lady is intent upon casting herself into the river!
Louise Come on, George! Now or never!

George joins them with his syringe rampant

George If you could contrive to hold her steady ...
Ron That's easier said than done!

Ron and Albert do their best to steady the struggling Donna

Donna Let me go! Let me go! Let me go!
Albert She sounds like a football supporter.
George I've had no experience of a moving target ...
Albert We're doing our best!
Ron I've got an arm! You take the waist!
Albert Oh, my God, I'm touching her!
Donna Tell that rapist to remove his hands!
Ron Hurry up, Doctor! We've got her steady! In you go!

George moves in for the kill

George Just a small prick ...
Ron Don't tell her that! *Now!*

Hidden by Ron, George injects with his syringe

Donna Aaaah!

After a moment, George stands back with his spent syringe. Donna's struggling subsides and she starts to go limp, supported like a rag doll on either side by Albert and Ron

Aah ... Aah ...

Ron There …! That's better, isn't it? All the anguish gone.
Donna (*dreamily*) Oh, yes … yes … yes …
Ron Come on, then — this way.

They help her towards the bedroom. She looks up at Ron, hopefully

Donna Are we heading for the bedroom?
Ron Yes. You need to lie down.
Donna (*sleepily*) That's what I've been telling you …

Albert opens the bedroom door

(*Looking about, happily*) Am I at a party? I *feel* as if I'm at a party. And what a lot of men …

She goes into the bedroom in a delighted daze

Albert closes the door. George dismantles his syringe and replaces it in his black bag. Ron approaches George, menacingly

Ron You've got a nerve coming here!

George looks up, surprised by his aggressive tone

George There was an emergency. You sent for me.
Ron Yes. But your services are required only as a physician. Not as an adulterer!
George That is impossible. I cannot *be* an adulterer.
Ron Why not? Have you sustained some lasting injury?
George I am unmarried.
Ron *She* isn't!
George The lady in the bedroom?
Ron The lady in here! This lady! She is married to *me*!
George (*sadly*) Ah — yes. Alas. I know that now. She told me in the kitchen over a comforting cup of sweet tea …
Albert (*to Ron*) Oh, dear. And you were trying to keep your marriage a secret … (*He grins*)

Ron glares at him

Louise *Were* you, Ronnie?
Ron Of course I wasn't! Why should I want to do that?
George (*crossing to Albert*) Ah! A pizza delivery boy! How fortunate. I seem to have worked up quite an appetite. Do you have anything with anchovies?

Albert Don't be daft! I haven't got any pizzas *with* me.

George Do you account yourself a failure, then? I would have thought a prerequisite of being a delivery boy was to have something to deliver.

Albert We only deal with orders! We don't carry samples about on the off-chance!

George Then can I place an order? Anything with anchovies will suit. Perhaps a little Parmesan …

Albert You can't order through me! I don't take orders! I only deliver!

Ron And he doesn't do *that* anymore now he's into high finance …

Albert My mother said that if I played my cards well one day I could be the Chancellor of the Exchequer.

Ron The rate *you're* going you'll soon be the Governor of the Bank of England. (*He turns to Louise, belligerently*) Your doctor friend hadn't got very far, had he?

Louise No. He was sitting in his car outside. And he's not my friend. He's just a doctor.

Ron He travelled all the way from London to see you! *And* with flowers!

Louise Of course he didn't!

Ron Then what's he doing here? And why was he still sitting outside in his car? Why hadn't he driven off towards London?

George I was plucking up courage.

Ron Are you a nervous driver?

George I purchased a modest quarter bottle of gin during my frantic search for flowers and secreted it in the glove compartment of my car.

Louise Oh, Doctor! You haven't been drinking *again*?

George I fear so, dear lady. Regretfully, a touch more courage was required.

Albert No wonder you had difficulty injecting into a moving target …!

Ron (*going to George*) And why was more courage required? Courage to do what?

The gin has done its work

George To return here and declare my passion for your wife!

Ron What?!

George You may consider me to be nothing but a stupid doctor, not well-versed in the ways of love, but I have long admired her in her rare visits to my consulting room.

Louise is appalled by such a revelation. Ron turns to glare at her

Ron He *is* your doctor! (*to George*) I'll have you struck off! (*To Louise*) So you *do* know him!

Louise Well ... yes. But in the consulting room he has always been the model
  of propriety.

Ron Well, he's making up for it now! How did you know she was here?

George I followed her from London ...

Ron (*to Louise*) You followed me, and he followed you?! We must have
  been in convoy!

George I could contain my passion for her no longer! (*He goes to Louise,
  passionately*)

Ron If I wasn't a tolerant man I should demand satisfaction! (*Glaring at
  Louise*) Well? What have you to say for yourself?

Louise suddenly begins to laugh. A reaction that surprises Ron

Louise Oh, darling! You're so *funny*!

Albert Yes, he is, isn't he? (*He laughs also*)

Louise Fancy you thinking he was — Oh dear, oh dear, oh dear! (*She laughs
  and laughs*)

Albert Oh dear, oh dear, oh dear! (*He also*)

Ron I'm glad you're both so easily amused.

Louise You don't really *believe* what the doctor's been telling you?

Ron I hope I have no reason to doubt the veracity of a member of the BMA.

Louise He didn't really come here to see *me*.

George Yes, I did! I did ...!

Louise covers his mouth with her hand, and then goes to Ron

Louise You said yourself that secrecy is essential if a man is to perform his
  duties satisfactorily. Don't you remember?

Ron Well, he didn't keep it a secret, did he? I found out!

Louise You misunderstood. The doctor's apparent obsession with love and
  his frantic search for flowers was only a cover for his *real* reason for being
  here.

Ron and Albert consider this for a moment

Albert (*to Ron*) I don't know what she's talking about.

Ron Neither do I ...!

George Neither do I ...

Louise Oh, dearest, have you forgotten?

Ron Forgotten what?!

Louise The river!

Ron River?

Louise Flowing under the bridge outside …
Ron (*a beat*) What?
Louise The sad trout floating on the surface …
Ron (*carefully*) W-what are you getting at?

Louise echoes Ron's own earlier exposition

Louise The golden sands that were once a paradise for toddlers … soon to be polluted beyond recognition …
Albert Ah! Pollution. Somebody mentioned that …
Ron But what's that got to do with the doctor?
George Perhaps I could go outside for a minute and check the level of my gin …
Louise That's why he's here! Because of the pollution!

Ron freezes for a second

Ron W-what?
Louise His flowers and his passion are only pretence. He's here to take samples from the river to test the levels of pollution! (*She smiles at him, triumphantly*)

Ron stares at her, uncertainly, his own lie having suddenly become reality. Then he crosses to George, smiling boldly, trying to carry it off

Ron Ha! Ha! Ha! Well, well, well! Good heavens, Doctor! You should have said! Why didn't you *tell* me what you came here for?
George I did! I came here to declare my passion for your wife! (*He goes on to his knees in front of Louise*)
Louise Doctor! Doctor! Please get up … (*She helps him to his feet, embarrassed*) You don't have to do that anymore.
George (*bemused*) Don't I?
Ron (*with a big smile*) If only I'd known before you arrived …!
Albert Why didn't you?

Ron glares at him, put off his stride by his intervention

Ron What?
Albert If you're the Minister for the Environment you should know all about pollution.
Louise Oh, he does. Don't you, dearest? That's why he's been visiting this bungalow so often — to find out which of the local factories have been emitting harmful by-products into the river and killing the fish.

Albert (*to Ron*) Is *that* what you told her? (*He laughs, noisily*)

Ron hits Albert, then turns, jovially, to George again

Ron I can't understand why you didn't come straight up to me when you arrived and say, "I've been sent here to test the levels of pollution", instead of scrabbling about on your knees with a bunch of flowers! Ha! Ha! Ha!
George I'm sorry. I don't think I ...
Louise He didn't know then that you were in charge of the operation!
Ron (*laughing, wildly*) I'm the Minister for the Bloody Environment! Of course I'm in charge of the operation!
Louise He probably thought it was top secret!
George (*unhappily*) That's what I *meant* it to be. I wasn't expecting all these people to be here ...

Albert nudges Ron, man-to-man

Albert Here — why don't you ask him what he's done with his equipment?

Ron stares at him, blankly, for a moment or two

Ron What?
Albert Well, surely he must have some equipment. If he's here to test the levels of pollution he can't do it with a bottle of gin, now can he?

Ron is, naturally, reluctant to pursue the matter

Ron Wh–what does it matter?
Albert Well, we ought to establish the facts.
Ron It ... it'll be in his car.
Albert In the boot?
Ron Yes.
Albert (*to George*) Is it?
George (*blankly*) Is it?
Albert In the boot!
George Oh, no. In the glove compartment. It's only a small bottle. It would be quite lost in the boot.
Albert Your equipment! Is it in the boot?
George I have boots in the boot.
Albert Wading boots?
George Wellington boots. And a gallon of petrol in a red can in case of emergency. (*He smiles, sagely, at Louise*) I like to be prepared.
Louise You must have been a Boy Scout.

Albert I don't believe a word of it!

Ron (*quietly*) Shut up …!

Louise Albert, I hope you're not suggesting that the doctor *made up* a story about pollution, are you?

Ron No! No — of course he isn't! (*He glares at Albert*)

Louise There *is* pollution in this area of Sussex, isn't there, Ronnie?

Ron Yes! Yes, of course there is!

Louise I mean, you'd need to have an incredible imagination to make up a story like that, wouldn't you?

Ron Er … yes … yes, I suppose you would … (*He laughs, nervously*)

Albert Well, *I* don't believe it!

Ron Nobody asked you!

Louise As if anyone would pretend there was pollution just to hide their own sexual adventures! (*She laughs at such a preposterous idea*)

Ron Yes — exactly! (*Turning to Albert*) *I* believe it!

Louise Only someone with a really guilty conscience would make up such a story …

Ron Yes — exactly! (*To Albert again*) *I* believe it!

Louise I mean, how could anyone think that this poor man is really seething with hidden passion?

And certainly the doctor, in despair, does not remotely resemble Casanova

Ron Of course he isn't! (*To Albert*) What a suggestion!

George But I am! I *am* …!

Louise (*stopping his mouth with her fingers*) It's all right. You don't have to pretend anymore …

Albert *I* didn't think there *was* any pollution around here …

Ron Shouldn't you be going back to Pizza Palace?

Albert I caught a trout in the river out here only last week …

Ron We don't want to hear about it!

Albert Very nice it was, too. Big brown trout. My mother grilled it for me with some fried potatoes and a few frozen peas. Didn't do me any harm …

Louise (*in wide-eyed innocence*) Albert, surely you're not suggesting that the Minister for the Environment and a respected doctor from London are not telling the truth?

Albert I wouldn't be surprised …!

Louise But if their stories of pollution are untrue what would that mean …?

Albert It'd mean there are a couple of sex maniacs on the loose! (*He laughs*)

Ron hits Albert as Louise turns to look at George in assumed horror. George smiles, modestly, pleased with the description, and sits in the armchair

And at that moment WPC Hackett climbs in through the open window and confronts them

Brenda Four blasts of a whistle and cries of "Rape!" have been reported. Where is the guilty party?

Ron (*going quickly to her*) Officer, you really must stop entering through windows. It's extremely unnerving.

Brenda That's the idea! The element of surprise is essential in police work. Ringing bells and banging on doors would be enough to alert even the most inept of criminals.

Louise Is there a criminal *here*?

Ron No, of course there isn't! (*To Brenda*) It was a mistake. The police are not required.

Brenda Four blasts of a whistle and cries of "Rape!" You call that a mistake? (*She goes to Albert, her eyes brightening*) Ah! The pizza delivery boy has returned! My visit is not entirely without pleasure.

Albert (*nervously*) I — I was just about to leave ... !

Brenda A sensible decision. Callow youth must be protected from the lustful excesses of this place. Excesses which are receiving such surprising approval from the Prime Minister ... (*She glares at Ron*)

Albert That's why I'm going ... !

Brenda Nobody may leave until I have investigated the crime! (*Then, sweetly*) Besides, I owe you for my pizza. (*Recalling with relish*) Spinach, tomato, mozzarella cheese, surmounted by a tender egg. Glorious!

George (*in a dream*) No anchovies? I'm very fond of anchovies ...

Albert (*to Brenda*) It's all right! You don't have to pay! It was a gift!

Brenda As an officer of the law I cannot accept gratuities. (*She gives him money from her purse*) Is that sufficient?

Albert Yes! Yes, that's fine!

Brenda (*hopefully*) You're sure I'm not still just a little in your debt?

Albert No fear!

Brenda The streets at night are full of danger to young men about on their own. If you wish, I can accompany you safely back to your place of rest.

Albert No, no! That won't be necessary!

Ron Officer, we needn't detain you any longer. I'm sure you have more urgent matters to attend to.

Brenda A crime has been reported. I am here to investigate, and investigate I shall!

George *What* crime?

WPC Hackett goes to George, who is sitting in a heap in the armchair

Brenda You appear to be a spent force, Doctor. No wonder you're sitting down. Your declaration of love in the kitchen has obviously paid dividends.

George Far from it! I was repulsed and banished to my car …
Albert (*laughing*) From where you sought solace in gin!
Brenda (*suspiciously*) Ah! So then you returned here, emboldened by
    alcohol to make a second, more violent attempt? (*To Ron*) A doctor from
    London is now apparently at the top of my list of suspects.
George Of what am I suspected?
Brenda Rape!
George No, no. I am a romantic, not a rapist.
Brenda We have only your word for that!
Louise No, no, Doctor! You're here to perform scientific research. Remember?

*George tries to remember. Brenda sees the flowers wrapped in newspaper,
and picks them up from the sofa*

Brenda I see there is a second bunch of flowers here. Does this hint at further
    excesses? And wrapped in the pages of a tabloid newspaper! Decadence
    knows no bounds.
Albert The Minister for the Environment gave them to me.
Ron Shut up! Shut up!
Brenda Is this true? You gave the boy flowers?
Ron Well … yes, but I can ——
Brenda Not content with having two *women* on the go, you have now turned
    your attentions to young men in uniform!
Louise *Two* women, Ronnie? What can she be talking about?
Ron She's confused!
Louise Surely you haven't been taking advantage of Donna after she kindly
    lent you her bungalow to carry out your fight against pollution?
Brenda Fight against it? He seems to be encouraging it! He is attempting to
    pollute the mind of this innocent boy by giving him flowers!
Ron You don't understand — !
Albert He gave me money, as well …
Brenda What?!

Ron hits Albert again

    (*To Albert*) Have no fear. The strong arms of the law are here to protect you.
    (*She holds out the strong arms of the law, hopefully*)
Albert No! I can look after myself!
George (*to Louise*) Dear lady, could we not return to the kitchen? I cannot
    speak of passion in a crowded room.

WPC Hackett stands foursquare and holds her arms aloft

Brenda Nobody leaves this room until I have solved the crime! (*She closes the window, abruptly, to prevent anyone escaping*)

Ron (*going to her*) But there *is* no crime!

Brenda You expect me to ignore a cry of rape?

Ron If a crime has been committed, where's the victim?

Brenda You raise a valid point. (*She looks about*) There is only one lady present apart from myself — and I, regretfully, am not a contender — and she does not appear to be in a state of sexual disarray. (*To Louise*) I assume it was not *you* who summoned help?

Louise Of course it wasn't!

Brenda (*to Ron*) Then where is the other lady?

Ron W–what other lady?

Brenda The lady who lives here! It must have been she who shouted rape. However unlikely a scenario that may seem to be …

Ron She's lying down in her bedroom.

Brenda Recovering from her ordeal, no doubt?

Ron There has been no ordeal!

Brenda sets off towards the bedroom door

And she doesn't wish to be disturbed. You can't go in there!

Brenda I would be failing in my duty if I did not check the possibility of foul play.

Brenda goes into the bedroom

Albert starts to go. Ron intercepts him

Ron Where are *you* off to?

Albert I'm not staying here to be falsely accused.

Ron (*quietly, to Albert*) You can't just take my money and run!

Albert Oh, yes, I can! I don't want to be handcuffed to that policeperson!

Albert races to the window. He cannot open it. It is stuck again. He pushes at it, desperately. Ron laughs. Albert starts to go towards the hall, but Ron intercepts him, neatly

Ron No, you don't, you little weasel!

In panic, Albert looks the other way, moves quickly to open a cupboard door and disappears inside

George (*puzzled*) Good heavens! The pizza delivery boy seems to have disappeared into a cupboard …

Donna comes, unsteadily, out of the bedroom, supported by Brenda. She is having great difficulty remaining awake

Donna People keep entering my bedroom in uniform … (*She looks about, sleepily*) Are we having a party? How delightful. Who is in charge of the drinks?

George *I* have a bottle of gin in the glove compartment of my car …

Donna Excellent! I'm sure I can contribute some tonic water and a small lemon.

Ron Don't give her anything to drink! She's frisky enough as it is!

Donna (*seeing him*) Oh, pigeon, don't be such a spoilsport. (*She reels a little*) Oooh! I'm afraid I'm a little sleepy …

Ron (*going to assist her*) You'd better sit down on the sofa.

Donna I'd rather lie down on the bed. (*She tries to embrace Ron*)

Ron eludes her clutches. She staggers a little. Brenda assists her to the sofa. She peers at Brenda, sleepily

Donna Why is this police officer interrupting my sleep? It feels like the middle of the night …

George Shall I go and fetch my gin?

Brenda Remain where you are! My investigations are not yet complete.

Donna Are you here to arrest somebody?

Brenda If the guilty party can be identified.

Donna Has a crime been committed, then?

Brenda Of course it has!

Donna Oh, Ronnie, you naughty boy, what *have* you been doing?

Ron I haven't been doing anything!

Donna Then let's go back to the bedroom and start …

Donna tries to get up, but Brenda restrains her and she sinks back on to the sofa

Ron (*to Louise*) She's still hallucinating! (*To Brenda*) I think we should allow her to return to her room alone. The poor woman is far too sleepy for sensible conversation.

Brenda No, no. I must hear her story immediately. The guilty party must be given no time to escape.

Donna (*peering at him*) Why is the good doctor still here?

Ron Ah. I — I asked him to return. There was an emergency.

Donna Really? I must have missed that … (*To George*) Please don't feel you have to stand on ceremony … take the object of your desire into the kitchen … (*she yawns*) … and continue your protestations of love … (*She falls asleep*)

George (*to Louise, smiling happily*) Dear lady, shall we proceed?

Louise Doctor — I told you! — this lovelorn act of yours is no longer necessary ...! (*She smiles, nervously, at Ron*)

Brenda pulls at the sleeping figure on the sofa, urgently

Brenda Don't go to sleep! I need to hear your evidence!

Donna stirs, sleepily

Donna Is it time to get up already? It seems far too early to contemplate cornflakes and kippers.

Brenda (*to Ron*) Help me to get her to her feet! We must walk her up and down. She must be kept awake at all costs!

Reluctantly, Ron assists her. They pull Donna to her feet, one on each side

Ron She doesn't want to be woken up! Why can't you let her sleep?

Brenda Come on, dear!

Donna Where are we going?

Brenda We're going for a walk!

Donna Oh. How nice. But is the sun shining? I'm strictly a fair weather pedestrian ... (*She tries, but cannot take a pace*)

Ron It's no good! She wishes to sleep!

George (*quietly, to Louise*) She has no choice. I have sedated her.

Brenda What did you say, Doctor?

Ron Officer, you really must allow her to return to her room!

Brenda We don't accept defeatism in the Sussex police. Come along — one foot in front of the other — left ... right ... left ... right ...

Supported by Ron and Brenda, Donna takes a few faltering steps

(*Looking about*) Where is the pizza boy? His fine strong young arms would come in useful ...

Ron Never mind! He'll be back in a minute!

Brenda (*smiling*) Ah — a call of nature. I understand.

George He's hiding in the cupboard.

Brenda What?!

Ron Take no notice. London doctors are famous for their sense of humour.

Brenda Left ... right ... left ... right ...

Donna Are you encouraging me to work up an appetite for breakfast?

Brenda We want to keep you awake!

Ron (*quietly*) No, we don't ...!

Donna (*sleepily*) We would have to walk some distance, I fear … before I could face up to cornflakes and kippers … oh … (*She slumps completely, and is only held up by Ron and Brenda*)

Ron It's no good! She'll have to sit down.

They sit Donna on the sofa again. She sighs with relief

Donna Oh, good … it was just a short stroll after all … (*She yawns*) Oh, dear … (*She closes her eyes*)

Brenda Black coffee! We'll have to give her black coffee. That should do the trick. (*She starts to go*)

Ron Surely your questioning can wait until later?

Brenda On the contrary. Speed is of the essence. The trail must not be allowed to cool. (*She glares at George*) I shall occupy the kitchen only for a moment. I know you are anxious to utilize it in the cause of lust!

Brenda goes into the kitchen

Donna stirs and opens her eyes, hopefully

Donna Has the policewoman gone in search of drink?

Ron (*sitting beside her*) No, no — she has duties to perform elsewhere. (*Singing to her*) "Go to sleep, close thine eyes, thou shalt see paradise …"

Donna Oh, Ronnie … (*She settles her head on his chest*)

Ron casts a helpless look at Louise, and continues to sing the lullaby

Ron "Go to sleep, close thine eyes, thou shalt see paradise …"

George (*suddenly activated*) My passion can be contained no longer! (*He falls on to his knees in front of Louise*)

Louise Doctor! I told you! It is no longer necessary for you to continue this charade! (*She tries to pull him to his feet*) Get up! Get up!

Albert looks out of the cupboard

Albert Has she gone yet?

He sees Ron, with Donna's head on his chest, singing a lullaby, and the Doctor on his knees in front of Louise. He cannot believe his eyes

Oh, my God …!

He disappears back into the cupboard

Ron (*singing*) "So good-night now once more, with roses roof'd o'er ..."
Louise Get up. Get up!

Brenda bustles back in from the kitchen with a cup of black coffee

Ron stops singing. Brenda sees George on his knees, and shudders with frustrated passion

Brenda Doctor, your passion is relentless ...

Louise succeeds in getting George back on his feet

(*Quietly, as she crosses to the sofa*) Would that my male colleagues in the Sussex Police were as uncontrollable ... Here is black coffee! We'll soon have her on her feet again.

Brenda hands the coffee to Ron, who puts it, reluctantly, to Donna's lips

(*Turning to George and Louise*) I have finished in the kitchen. I suggest you secrete yourselves in there in the interests of decorum. (*Quietly, to herself*) I could not bear to witness the event which appears to be imminent ... (*She shudders with envy*)

Ron empties the coffee into a potted plant. Brenda turns to see how he is getting on and sees the empty cup

Brenda Good heavens! She has a startling capacity for coffee. (*She goes back towards the kitchen, hesitating near the others*) I fear you will have to delay your declaration of love for another moment.

She goes into the kitchen

George goes on to his knees, and Ron starts to sing again, softly

Ron "All tied up with bows, slip under the clothes ..."
Louise Get up! Get up! (*She struggles with him*)

Albert comes out of the cupboard, sees them still at it, and goes quickly to the window. But he cannot open it. It is still stuck. He races back into the cupboard and closes the door, quietly. Brenda returns with a fresh cup of black coffee

Ron stops singing. Brenda looks at George on his knees

Brenda Your passionate persistence is admirable ...

Louise pulls George to his feet. Brenda arrives at the sofa

Reinforcements!

She hands the cup to Ron, who holds it, tentatively, to Donna's lips. She sips some of it, and murmurs, sleepily

Donna Hmm ... hmm ... oh, Ronnie ...

Brenda She is reviving! (*She turns to the others*) All clear in the kitchen now. You may proceed.

Ron empties the coffee into the potted plant again. Brenda turns to find the cup is empty again

Ah! Her consumption of coffee is most encouraging.

Ron It's no good! She must be left to sleep in peace. The coffee is having no effect.

Brenda I can only assume it is decaffeinated. I shall try a further cup. (*She goes, briskly, to the kitchen, saying to the others as she passes*) Contain yourselves a moment longer.

She goes into the kitchen

Ron starts to sing the lullaby again. George goes on to his knees. Louise tries to stop him

Ron "Go to sleep, close thine eyes, thou shalt see paradise ..."

Louise Get up! Get up!

The cupboard door opens very slightly, and Albert peers out and then hastily withdraws. Brenda returns with further coffee

Ron stops singing. Louise pulls George to his feet, so they appear to be embracing. Brenda glances at them as she passes, shudders but says nothing, and hastens across to Ron again

Brenda One final cup and then to work!

Ron takes the cup and puts it to Donna's lips. She sips a little. Brenda looks about

The pizza delivery boy seems to be spending above average time about his ablutions ...

Ron empties the coffee into the potted plant again. Brenda turns and sees the cup is empty again

Good heavens! Her capacity for coffee exceeds even the doctor's capacity for love! (*She starts to pull Donna to her feet*) Come along, then, dear!
Donna (*sleepily*) Are we going for another walk?
Brenda Just a short one.
Donna What a pity. I was quite comfortable in this gentleman's arms. (*She smiles at Ron*) Perhaps we can soon go into the bedroom together …

Ron looks at Louise, helplessly

Ron She's had far too much coffee! Caffeine can affect the memory.

Supported on either side by Ron and Brenda as before, Donna essays a few halting steps

Brenda Now — one foot in front of the other — left … right … left … right …

Albert looks out of the cupboard again

He sees the extraordinary sight of three people, arm-in-arm, pacing with increasing speed about the room

He looks astonished, goes back inside quickly and slams the door

Brenda hears it

What was that?
Ron I didn't hear anything!
George (*intrigued*) He looked out of the cupboard …
Brenda What?! (*She looks towards the cupboard*)
Ron You see what I mean about the humour of the medical profession!
Brenda I shall investigate. The guilty party may still be on the premises.

Brenda opens the cupboard door with a flourish

Albert is revealed

Ah! This cupboard conceals a delightful surprise! I fear you have been searching for the bathroom in entirely the wrong area.
Albert I'm a stranger to this bungalow and unfamiliar with its geography.

Donna sees Albert, and recalls her dreadful experience at his hands

Donna Ah! There he is! *Now* I remember … Rape! Rape! (*She clings on to Ron in despair*)

George (*to Louise*) I've never known a rapist hide in a cupboard before.

Louise It may be standard practice in Sussex.

Ron You'd better sit down after your dreadful experience.

Ron sits her on the sofa again anxious to be out of her clutches, although she would have preferred to remain in his arms

Brenda So *you* are the one whose cry for help was reported by an alert neighbour?

Donna I was attempting to escape …

Brenda So a rape has been committed?

Donna (*thinking hard*) It is possible. But I fell asleep quite unexpectedly and am therefore unaware of the final outcome. (*Her eyelids droop*)

Brenda What a moment to miss through slumber …

Ron Officer, no crime has been committed!

Donna (*sleepily*) He cast himself upon me on the sofa …

Albert No, I didn't!

Brenda (*quietly*) Why am *I* never on the receiving end of such advances …?

Donna (*faintly*) Rape … rape … rape … . (*She goes back to sleep*)

Ron Don't you understand? This boy is in love with her!

Albert I'm getting out of here …! (*He starts to go*)

Brenda You will remain here until I have completed my investigations.

Ron (*going to Albert, threateningly*) Yes — and it's possible you may be accompanying this lady to the police station, handcuffed together in the back of a slow-moving van!

Albert Oh, my God …!

Ron So tell her the truth, you stupid boy! (*To Brenda*) He has long sustained a burning passion for this lady. His visits here — ostensibly to deliver pizzas that nobody ordered — were clearly a cover for his deeper desire. He loves her! And, I suspect, has done so for some time.

Albert No, I haven't …!

Ron (*quietly, to Albert*) Yes, you have, you little toad, and you've got *my* money to prove it!

Brenda She will confirm this when she wakes?

Ron You can hardly expect a lady to announce a love affair to all and sundry! But I can assure you that this boy has been carrying on with her for some weeks.

Brenda In that case, perhaps you can explain something!

She moves with heavy tread to the table on which stands the ornament. With dramatic effect, she lifts the lid and produces the hidden knickers, holding them aloft for all to see. General astonishment

Louise Ah! So that's where they got to!

George Underwear hidden in an ornament? Is this also standard practice in Sussex?

Donna What are my knickers doing inside an ornament ...?

Louise *Yours*?

Brenda (*to Ron*) If what you say about this poor boy is true, why were this lady's knickers in *your* pocket and not *his*?

Louise Ronnie ... isn't that extraordinary? Those knickers belong to Donna ... (*She considers the implications*)

Ron D–do they?

Donna Why is your friend so interested in my underwear?

Albert (*laughing*) She's not his friend. She's his wife!

Ron stares at him, a beaten man

Ron Now why did you have to go and say that?

Albert (*indicating the ladies*) Well, if I'm going to be her lover — you're going to be her husband!

Donna staggers to her feet and faces Ron, teetering gently

Donna Your wife! You never told me she was that!

Ron I didn't think it would help.

Donna sets off, unsteadily towards the bedroom

Where are you going?

Donna To my bedroom ...

Ron Ah — yes! What a good idea! You have a nice sleep! We'll try not to disturb you.

Donna goes into the bedroom

Louise (*thinking hard*) Ronnie ...

Ron Y–yes, darling?

Albert Can I go now, please?

Brenda I'm afraid not. I shall require you for further questioning. Which can either take place at the police station or in the privacy of my flat, whichever you prefer ...

Albert But I haven't done anything!
Brenda That is beside the point.

Donna returns, holding a brown envelope aloft. Ron hastens to her,
apprehensively

Ron Why have you returned? I thought you were anxious for sleep.
Donna I have something to show to your wife.
Ron What?!
Donna Being married to the Minister for the Environment, I am sure she has
   an eye for … natural photography …
Ron You wouldn't! You couldn't!
Donna Could — and would! (*She staggers off to Louise*)
George The sedative I administered seems to be wearing off …
Ron (*intervening*) Give those to me!
Donna No. I shall give them to your wife! (*She hands the envelope to Louise*)
   I'm sure she will find them of interest.
Louise Photographs? How nice. I always enjoy photographs. (*She sits on the
   sofa to look at them*)
Ron You won't enjoy these …!
Louise Are they holiday snaps?
Ron Not exactly, no …!
Brenda If those are the pictures you intend showing to the Prime Minister
   and his cabinet, I may have to confiscate them in the interests of public
   decency.
Ron (*hovering over Louise*) It's getting late! We should be going! And you
   know how you hate looking at other people's holiday snaps!
Louise (*well-mannered as always*) Ronnie, I shall have to take a quick look.
   It would be very rude not to. (*She looks at the first picture, and is puzzled*)
   I don't know what *that* is … (*She turns it the other way up, and laughs*)
   Good heavens! I didn't recognize it at first!
Ron (*anxiously*) W–what is it?
Louise It's a pizza.
Ron
Donna } (*together*) A *what*?!
Louise It's a picture of a pizza.

George looks up, hopefully

George Does it have anchovies?
Donna Let me see that … (*She sits beside Louise, takes the picture from her,
   looks at it and reacts*) It's a pizza!
Louise I told you it was. (*She looks at the next picture*) And here's another

one! (*Reading*) "Pepperoni, mushroom and onion with a spicy beef topping".

Ron Give them to me! (*He snatches the pictures and looks through them quickly, smiling with growing relief*) They're all pizzas! Pictures of pizzas! Well, well, well! Ha, ha, ha!

Brenda (*totally lost*) Why should you think that the Prime Minister would want to see pictures of pizzas …?

Ron What are you talking about?

Louise Albert, *you*'d be interested in these!

Albert (*man-of-the-world*) No, no. *I*'ve seen pictures of pizzas *before* …

Ron What?

Ron looks at Albert, a light beginning to dawn

Louise Donna … I don't understand. Why were you so keen to show me pictures of pizzas?

Donna is still sleepy and confused

Donna They weren't pictures of pizzas *then* … .

Louise Sorry?

Donna Those aren't *my* pictures!

Louise Then whose pictures are they?

Donna And how did they get into my bedroom …?

Ron darts another look at Albert, who gives a little smile and then tries, without success, to hide his guilt by looking at the ceiling

Louise So where are the pictures you *wanted* to show me?

Donna That's what *I*'d like to know …

Ron looks at Donna enthusiastically, a large smile of relief on his face

Ron You must have mislaid them! Yes! Of course! Ha! Ha! Ha! That's what happened. You mislaid them!

Donna I could have sworn I put them in that brown envelope …

Ron Well, you couldn't have done, could you? Ha! Ha!

Donna Oh, I shall find them, pigeon. I shall find them …

Ron (*quietly*) I don't think you will …! (*He chuckles, triumphantly, and casts a grateful glance towards Albert*) Ha! Ha! Ha!

Donna starts to go towards the kitchen. Ron sees her

Now where are you off to?

Donna Into the kitchen. I think I need a cup of black coffee.
Brenda *Another* one?!

Donna stops at the kitchen door and looks back, having noticed George as she passed. Her spirits start to rise

Donna Perhaps *you*'d care for a cup, Doctor? I'd hate your desperate drive from London to be completely fruitless. And from what I know about you, we may find we have more than coffee in common ...

Donna goes, unsteadily, into the kitchen

George What did she mean by that?
Ron I should go and find out!

The kitchen door reopens, and Donna reaches back in and pulls George, abruptly, out into the kitchen and slams the door

Louise rises in surprise. She and Brenda watch them go, then look at each other in astonishment. Ron turns to Albert. Unseen by the ladies, and with deft dexterity, Ron produces another ten-pound note and Albert produces the missing pictures. They make the exchange neatly, put their respective spoils back into their pockets and shake hands, smiling happily. Albert goes to Brenda

Albert *Now* am I free to go, Officer?
Brenda Certainly. (*He starts to go*) But I shall accompany you.
Albert What?!
Brenda The streets of Sussex are full of hidden dangers for young men travelling alone. (*She closes to him, heavy with desire*) And on the way perhaps we could stop for a ... (*she draws in her breath, noisily*) ... large pizza?
Albert W–what had you in mind?
Brenda Spinach, tomato, mozzarella cheese, surmounted by a tender egg. Glorious!
Albert Oh, my God ...!

Albert runs for his life out into the hall, with Brenda in hot pursuit, blowing her whistle as she goes

Ron and Louise are alone. Music fades in softly

Louise Ronnie ...?

Ron Y–yes, darling…?

Louise There's something I don't understand…

Ron Oh, surely not!

Louise picks up the knickers with the tips of her fingers and holds them up in front of him, swinging them gently like a pendulum

Louise How on earth did Donna's knickers end up on the pavement in the middle of Oxford Street?

Ron I … I'm sure there must be a perfectly good explanation …

Louise (*smiling, icily*) Well, perhaps you'll be able to think of one on the way home.

Ron Yes — right … (*He hastens to the window and, to his surprise, opens it quite easily*) It opened!

Louise Why shouldn't it open? It's a window.

Ron Well, it doesn't usually! (*He smiles, hopefully*) Perhaps it's an omen? Perhaps my luck's going to change?

Louise shakes her head

Louise No, pigeon. Your luck just ran out!

She drops the knickers into his hands and goes out through the window

Ron is about to follow her when the potted plant suddenly wilts and collapses, sated with black coffee. He looks at it for a second, worried by the obvious symbolism, then hastily casts the knickers aside and starts to climb out of the window as the music swells and ——

—— the CURTAIN *falls*

FURNITURE AND PROPERTY LIST

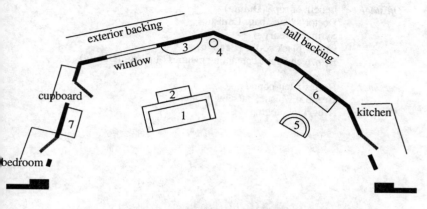

1 sofa   2 sofa table   3 crescent table   4 pot plant   5 armchair
6 shelf/cupboard unit   7 desk

ACT I

On stage: Sofa
Sofa table. *On it*: potted plant (collapsible), china dish with lid
Armchair
Desk
Bookshelf/cupboard unit. *On shelf*: vase of flowers, newspaper
Crescent table. *On it*: whistle, ornaments
Potted plants
Window curtains open

Off stage: Various parcels (**Donna**)
Box of pizza (**Albert**)
Thermos flask, packet of sandwiches (**Donna**)
Bunch of flowers (**George**)

Personal: **Ron**: latchkey
Louise: handbag containing pair of panties
Brenda: notebook
Louise: handkerchief

ACT II

Set: Glass of water for **Louise**

Re-set: Whistle on crescent table

Off stage: Length of rope (**Donna**)
                Doctor's black bag (**Louise**)
                Syringe (**George**)
                Cup of black coffee (**Brenda**)
                Brown envelope containing pictures of pizzas (**Donna**)

Personal: **Ron**: six ten-pound notes
                Brenda: whistle, purse with money
                Albert: photographs

LIGHTING PLOT

Property fittings required: nil.

Interior. The same scene throughout

ACT I. Afternoon

To open: General lighting with sunshine effect through window

Cue 1   **Ron** turns to attend to his wife   (Page 39)
           Black-out

ACT II. Afternoon

To open: General lighting with sunshine effect through window

No cues

EFFECTS PLOT

ACT I

ACT II